MW01614155

52 THINKS II

52 THINKS II
Copyright © 2025 by Phillip T. Hopersberger

Cover Design:
Peter Ashford Hopersberger

Website:
www.TotallyWriteousCopy.com

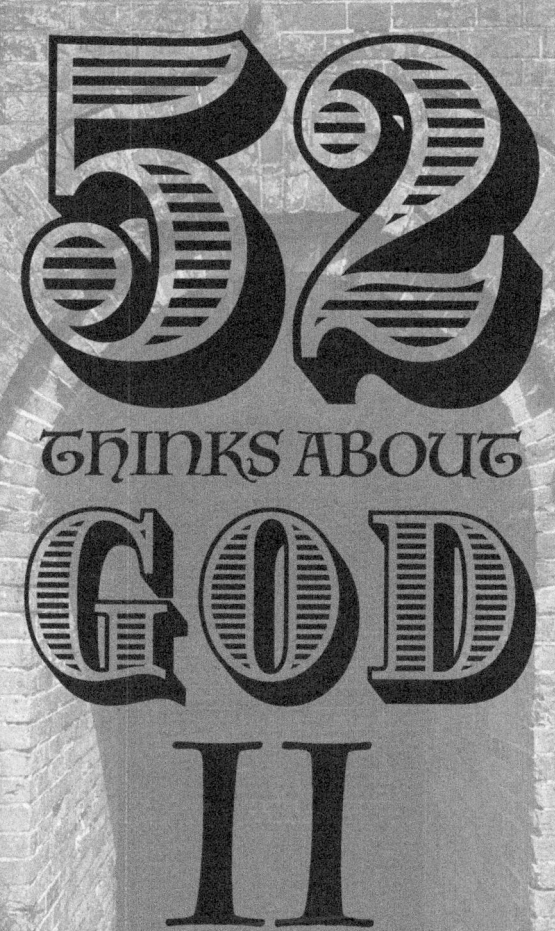

52

THINKS ABOUT

GOD

II

Two-Minute Reads Each Week
for the Whole Year About God

A DEVOTIONAL BY

PHILLIP T. HOPERSBERGER

PUBLISHED BY
SHAKESPEARE'S IN THE ALLEY

*"Like one, that on a lonesome road
Doth walk in fear and dread,
And having once turned round walks on,
And turns no more his head;
Because he knows, a frightful fiend
Doth close behind him tread."*

(The Rime of the Ancient Mariner)

*"Since then the children share in flesh and blood, He Himself
likewise also partook of the same, that through death He might
render powerless him who had the power of death, that is, the devil;
and might deliver those who through fear of death were subject to
slavery all their lives."*

(Hebrews 2:14-15)

"Oh, oh, oh!" cried the two girls, rushing back to the Table.

"Oh, it's too bad," sobbed Lucy; "they might have left the body alone."

"Who's done it?" cried Susan. "What does it mean? Is it more magic?"

"Yes!" said a great voice behind their backs. "It is more magic." They looked round. There, shining in the sunrise, larger than they had seen him before, shaking his mane (for it had apparently grown again) stood Aslan himself.

"Oh, Aslan!" cried both the children, staring up at him, almost as much frightened as they were glad.

"Aren't you dead then, dear Aslan?" said Lucy.

"Not now," said Aslan.

"You're not—not a—?" asked Susan in a shaky voice. She couldn't bring herself to say the word "ghost." Aslan stooped his golden head and licked her forehead. The warmth of his breath and a rich sort of smell that seemed to hang about his hair came all over her.

"Do I look it?" he said.

"Oh, you're real, you're real! Oh, Aslan!" cried Lucy and both girls flung themselves upon him and covered him with kisses.

"But what does it all mean?" asked Susan when they were somewhat calmer.

"It means," said Aslan, "that though the Witch knew the Deep Magic, there is a magic deeper still which she did not know. Her knowledge goes back only to the dawn of Time. But if she could have looked a little further back, into the stillness and darkness before Time dawned, she would have read there a different incantation. She would have known that when a willing victim who had committed no treachery was killed in a traitor's stead, the Table would crack and Death itself would start working backward."

– C.S. Lewis, *Chronicles of Narnia*

Introduction

Some people have a knack for writing and get our attention after just a few words. They weave spells in our mind as we drift away to a far-off realm or recall an experience from our past that brings a moment back to life. Somehow, such wordsmiths grab our interest and make us want to read further. On top of that, if they hit a topic of great appeal to us, then we're hooked! We have no choice but to follow along, and like Narnia's fabled wardrobe…go even further in.

Phil Hopersberger is that kind of writer. He's worked at his craft for years, in different venues and handling various subjects. He'll be telling a story about his rough fighting days while growing up in a Detroit high school, and then out of nowhere pops a succinct moral to the story, just like one of *Aesop's Fables!* These processes have sharpened and honed his pen, as well as his mind. Or is it the other way around? Was his mind growing before finding the proper expressions in his pen? I'm not sure!

For example, writing the initial volume of his *52 Thinks About God* in 2021, he presented 52 devotional meditations that take two minutes each to read, one per week. This initial installment treats the subject of Christmas. Does this great event have more in common with Charles Dickens' character Scrooge or with Charlie Brown? Phil's answer may surprise you in the very first lesson. Scrooge, of course! Really? Why? You'll know by the end of his *Think* after working through that brief lesson.

Lesson 35 of *52 Thinks* concerns death. How do Bob Dylan's songs help with this most jolting subject? Then the reader is hit rather unexpectedly with the ultimate truth that ties together Dylan and death—Jesus Christ's death, His resurrection, and immortality for those who trust Him.

This last subject is at the very crux of the present Easter installment of *52 Thinks About God II*, also consisting of two-minute meditations. Imagine actually meeting the rock and roll star Alice Cooper and having him sign one of your *52 Thinks* books? That happened to Phil. Wow, that would be cool! Then, without warning, Jesus Christ emerges from this true story. But you'll have to read it for yourself!

Talk about Alice Cooper, how about the entry from *52 Thinks II* with Phil seeing Ozzy Osbourne and the *Black Sabbath* crew? What? That turns to the gospel message as well, tying together JFK, Ozzy, and the Son of God...the real "Iron Man!"

52 Thinks II is all about the gospel message of the deity, death, and resurrection of Jesus Christ, the Savior of the world. As Phil wrote to me once regarding this book, *"I'd say Easter is the framework of the house that I'm hanging everything on as far as a theme."* Like Jerusalem's empty tomb, and Narnia's magical wardrobe, *52 Thinks II* lights up that same spot. Why not take a peek inside for yourself? In the back of tomb and wardrobe, in the dark, is a whole new world where He is risen!

Gary Habermas, Ph.D.

Distinguished Research Prof of Apologetics & Philosophy
School of Divinity
Liberty University

www.GaryHabermas.com

From the Author

Every Easter, I watch *Jesus of Nazareth* (1977) starring Robert Powell. Franco Zeffirelli directed some dynamite scenes, but my favorite — and the one that answers Susan's, *"But what does it all mean?"* to a resurrected Aslan in *Chronicles of Narnia* — is the scene where Jesus tells a story at Matthew's house party (Luke 15:11-32). Watch it and decide for yourself.

This sequel to *52 Thinks About God* (2021) is more of my newspaper columns intended to help you answer Susan's "was dead" query. Her six words are deathbed critical. It's the life-question you must answer. Like death, no one gets a pass. Read a Think a week and decide for yourself.

Gary Habermas graciously agreed to write the Introduction. He's spent his *"facts are stubborn things"* life proving Easter and his work is a gift I hope you'll unwrap (his website is packed with free information). What do you have to lose, maybe a few hours? Check him out and decide for yourself.

So if Jesus is God, died for your sin, and rose again, so what? For me, five gears clicked into place…immortality, knowing my Creator as a friend, a clear conscience, real peace, and death is no longer a flimsy trapdoor. Death is now a doorknob to turn and see my King (like Peter Jackson's ending in *LOTR* (2003) with Aragorn's coronation, receiving his bride, and honoring his friends).

These columns were written over many years, so not every one is about Easter, but Easter is the every day bedrock (like the Christmas theme in *52 Thinks About God*). The Incarnation and Easter are literally nailed together.

I suggest you look up the Bible verses for yourself (get an easy to read Bible like the *NLT, ESV,* or *NIV* version. I like the *NASB*). If the Bible is new to you, the first number is the book chapter, and the next number is the verse in that chapter. So, Matthew 22:1-14 is Matthew chapter 14, verses 1 to 14.

Another favorite scene is at the end of Zeffirelli's film when Nicodemus (Laurence Olivier) quotes the Isaiah 53 Messiah prophecy. We met Nicodemus earlier in the "born again" scene (John 3:1-16), and Jesus' words click for him as he watches Jesus die. Watch it for yourself and decide. I hope His words click for you too (Jeremiah 29:12-13). He is in fact...risen!

Week 1:
Jesus Doesn't Use A Surfboard

"You are mistaken...greatly mistaken (Mark 12:24, 27)."

What's impossible…Time Travel maybe? Physicists say there are 11 dimensions (we perceive only time, depth, width, and height), and some say as many as 26 dimensions. That means we could walk to Chicago from Grand Rapids…on top of Lake Michigan, and Peter's stroll with Jesus over the Sea of Galilee isn't so impossible.

Most dismiss that hike as a fable (despite 12 eyewitnesses). Ask any leper; Jesus was all about the impossible. As God, He created the Laws of Physics. I think Jesus inspired Lewis Carroll's exchange with Alice and the White Queen in *"Through the Looking Glass."*

"Alice laughed. 'There's no use trying,' she said. 'One can't believe impossible things.'

'I daresay you haven't had much practice,' said the Queen. 'When I was your age, I always did it for half an hour a day. Why, sometimes I've believed as many as six impossible things before breakfast.'" Charles Dodgson (Lewis Carroll was his pen name) wrote, *"I owe all to Him who loved me, and died on the Cross of Calvary."* So…

Just because you haven't seen it, doesn't mean it's impossible. The Bible names this "yet unseen" stuff – Faith. Does a water-walk still sound crazy? How about sky-walking? Before 1903 walking in the sky was impossible, but today millions will get out of their seats and walk in the aisles on thousands of airplanes…without a thought of impossible.

So is impossible really that…impossible? Is only seeing believing? Have you seen your brain? Inspected your brakes before each trip? Such unseen realities (impossibles) aren't so far-fetched anymore. Physics has caught up with God's written record of impossible.

The Bible oozes with Quantum Physics…floating ax heads, walks through walls, cold furnaces, the sun standing still, even talking donkeys. Just made up like Lewis' chatty white rabbit…or realities

where Mr. Possible got punched in the nose? This question got answered unequivocally on the day impossible was erased – a dead man opened His eyes!

You may scoff at Easter, but for more than a month the wet-walk witnesses and others saw Jesus alive (Acts 1:3), over 500 of them! Even a religious expert who murdered Jewish-Christians saw Him (Acts 9), who then believed impossible. Later, as an Apostle, Paul said most of the 500 were still alive if they wanted to verify it (1 Corinthians 15:6).

Mark said (chapter 12 above) that the religious experts foolishly tried to trip up Jesus about the resurrection of the dead (they'd never seen it, so didn't believe it). He told them they were dead wrong about *"understanding the Scriptures and the power of God."* Not only mistaken, but greatly mistaken. That hurt, but could His words apply to you?

Consider Jesus' impossible story – a dead man in flaming agony wants to warn his five brothers to repent and believe to avoid his awful fate (Luke 16:19-31). That's impossible now, He said. *"If they do not listen to Moses and the Prophets (the Bible), neither will they be persuaded if someone rises from the dead."* I can hear your doubt-grumbles…

"That's as crazy as a talking white rabbit who wants to sell me the Son of God's surfboard – Never Used. Or that I'll be raised from the dead and have to give an account for my life (2 Corinthians 5:10; Hebrews 9:27).*"* Yeah, you're right. That's impossible.

Week 2:
12 to 3

"Was it not necessary... (Luke 24:26)?"

Once a year, at noon, my Mom would make me come inside and sit quietly until 3PM, respectfully, because this was when Jesus was *"dying on the cross."* And not just dying, He was dying for me. That was *Good Friday* in our house.

School was out, so we usually played football in the street, that is, until she called me home. I could read or watch television, as long as I was reverent. To my Mother, it was necessary to honor Him. This made a deep impression; I mattered to God, to an innocent man, as Pontius Pilate said of the Jew who claimed to be God, who was murdered for me.

My Mother's parenting seems strange today since most folks ignore *Good Friday.* If she were not blind, we'd have driven to church, but this was her best attempt at worship to remember Jesus. Today is *Good Friday,* and I always feel weird about it. Should I be sad, be like everyone else as if nothing has happened, or be happy He died for me? What's necessary now?

Necessary is a funny word (writers are like this, drilling down on words and their meaning). It means *"essential, absolutely required."* And this is what Jesus said after His death in chapter 24 of Luke's resurrection account, *"Was it not necessary?"*

What does God have to do that is *"essential"* and *"absolutely required?"* This is very deep stuff if you think hard about it. What is demanded of God, by Himself, that is necessary? Make sure Jupiter spins? The sun sets on time all over the world? Judge sin fairly? What must be done, no matter what, by God's self-imposition on Himself?

I submit that Jesus dying a horrible, painful, and bloody, flesh-ripped death was necessary for God because of one inescapable thing...God loved us. And loved you personally, enough to become sin and be separated from His Father for the first time, take your judgment, one you deserved for your sin, all to get you back home, safe and sound.

He thought it necessary – essential, absolutely required, no other way to do it, the only way – because He loved you so very much, He'd even die just for you. That means if you were the only person on the planet, He would have died for your sins. Necessary? Wow! If I were God I'd have found another way, but apparently it was the only way possible. His love for you made this the only way to save you. Jesus said, *"I am the way* (John 14:6)."* Not a way, but the way. The only way. The necessary way to pay for sin.

The irony of this demand God put on Himself is what you choose to do with it. You can ignore Him. You don't have to come home (repent) and acknowledge what He did for you with your reverence. Stay outside and play football, as my friends did when my Mom called. Necessary doesn't apply to you. Necessary only applies to Good Friday, when His love for you was His *"necessary"* because you mattered enough to die for.

Week 3:
Saving Normandy

"For I, too, am a man under authority, with soldiers under me... (Matthew 8:9)."

A cigar clenched in his teeth, Captain Frank Lillyman leaped from a C-47 into a 120 mph wind, into darkness, and into history … the first American soldier, from Skaneatele, New York, landed in Normandy! That was 80 years ago this month, and it still impresses me.

The 17 paratroopers under Lillyman's command found themselves safe on French soil, but with only scant minutes to set up their *Eureka* radar equipment (in a church steeple) and lay out the massive "T" landing-lights for the hundreds of paratroopers already en route to liberate Europe … but they had a huge problem. They were a mile off course.

In 30 minutes the skies would be jammed with planes emptying the main body of troops looking for where his *Pathfinders* wanted them to jump. There was no time to get to their original spot. Frank decided the war would start right here and his men leapt into action.

When Frank gave an order, they obeyed it. No matter how difficult, *Pathfinders* find a way to get the job done, but what if his men had refused? What if they disobeyed his order and wanted to risk a double-time mile march to their original Drop Zone A? Fat chance. They were men *"under authority"* and trained to obey Frank's every word.

Matthew records another "Lillyman" soldier (with 100 men under his command) looking for Jesus to heal his servant, but he didn't want Him to come to his home to do it. The Roman Centurion sent his friends with this message, *"Just say the word and my servant will be healed."* Jesus marveled, *"I have not found such great faith in all of Israel."*

If you look between the lines, you'll see that Jesus was looking too (*"not found"* means He was searching), and He found "it" in a Gentile…a Roman invader who understood submission. This man recognized Jesus as God, and His authority. He knew Jesus' word was enough. He didn't need to see it (Luke 7:1-10), and that faith impressed Jesus!

Being *"under authority"* on June 6, 1944 saved thousands of soldier's lives and millions of European civilians. Frank obeyed his commander and jumped out of a perfectly good airplane. His men obeyed him and found new fields for paratroopers to land on. Despite the danger, being under authority is a safe place, especially if it's under God's Word.

Isaiah 66:2 and 2 Chronicles 16:9 say that God is still looking for something today (you can discover "it" yourself, unless you're too busy to read God's Word, which should tell you a lot about whose authority you're under). Jesus made it simple to know if you are under His authority when He said, *"And why do you call Me, 'Lord, Lord,' and do not do what I say* (Luke 6:46)?*"* His words, His will for you, are revealed in the Bible's pages.

In 80 years (2104), like Frank Lillyman, you won't be here. You will have jumped into darkness, into history, and into eternity too. Where will you land? I hope it's looking at a smiling Jesus, amazed at your Centurion-like faith (1 John 5:11-13). Will you submit to Him, impress Him? Here's to your safe jump and a saved landing, *"under authority."*

Week 4:
Lincoln's Funambulist

"If righteousness comes through the Law, then Christ
died needlessly (Galatians 2:21)."

Henry Colcord, is a name you should know, believe me. He managed Charles Blondin who walked from the United States to Canada for the very first time…on a tightrope…strung over Niagara Falls! Blondin was the greatest funambulist in 1859!

That first crossing was 165 years ago. Charles did it many times… backwards, at night, stopping to take a picture, doing flips (backwards), with a bag over his head, pushing a wheelbarrow, and he even carried a stove on his back and cooked an omelet (that he lowered on a rope to the passengers on the *Maid of the Mist* boat 160 feet below)!

When Lincoln ran for President in 1860, *Harper's Weekly* depicted him in a cartoon as Blondin over Niagara Falls carrying a slave on his shoulders. This mockery was based in truth because Henry Colcord actually did this on Blondin's shoulders…more than once!

On one occasion a wide-eyed boy witnessed Blondin and Henry's jaunt. The King of the Rope saw him and said, *"Do you believe I could do that with you?"* The stunned boy could only nod. *"Hop on,"* Charles said, *"and I'll carry you across too."* The boy backed away. *"Not on your life!"* He believed in the Frenchman, but he didn't put his trust in him.

Nowhere is this gap of comprehending genuine faith more vast than in what you do with Jesus Christ. Without an eternal, saving trust in His death and resurrection (compared to a head nod belief to an historical fact), you are not truly seated on His bloody shoulders. Trust is a heart thing and it means action. Belief is a head thing, safely tucked away.

There's another chasm, a gorge that separates us from God, and it's wider than the 1,110 feet Blondin strolled. *"But your iniquities have made a separation between you and your God, and your sins have hidden His face from you so that He does not hear* (Isaiah 59:2)." We "believe" we can ford this spiritual Grand Canyon by our good deeds, but…

Isaiah 64:6 says, *"All our righteous deeds are like a filthy garment."* Our Sunday best is like my mechanic's overalls, soaked by three decades of grease and oil. He'd never wear that to a wedding, but that's exactly what we do in our pride, thinking we're pretty good underneath the grime. God would welcome us to Heaven, right? But Matthew 22:1-14...

"Jesus spoke to them again in parables, saying, 'The kingdom of heaven may be compared to a king who gave a wedding feast for his son. And he sent out his slaves to call those who had been invited to the wedding feast, and they were unwilling to come.'"

They made excuses, attacked his servants, and proved unworthy...so he invited strangers.

"But when the king came in to look over the dinner guests, he saw a man there who was not dressed in wedding clothes, and he said to him, 'Friend, how did you come in here without wedding clothes?' And the man was speechless. Then the king said to the servants, 'Bind him hand and foot, and throw him into the outer darkness; in that place there will be weeping and gnashing of teeth.'"

Seems harsh, but this intruder was soaked in oily pride. He had insulted the king. *"I'm my own man and I will do what I please. I don't need your approval. I'm good enough without your clothes."* He thumbed his nose at the king's generosity and his sovereignty. You are that man, if you think you're good enough without God's provision of His Son.

This intruder believed he was fine, but he was not dressed properly (Isaiah 61:10). The boy "believed," but was unwilling. Henry (and Lincoln's slave) knew they were helpless and just stepped out in genuine faith (Ephesians 2:8-9). They heard His invitation, *"Hop on and I'll carry you...(on) a cross."* They got it...the Kingdom of Rope has a kind King.

Week 5:
Sipping Eyes and Slurping Ears

"The heavens are telling, their expanse is declaring...
(but) there is no speech, nor are there words;
their voice is not heard (Psalm 19)."

Any guess what animal has the best hearing? Most would say a bat, but it's actually the lowly moth. The *Greater Wax Moth* has the best hearing of all. Their very life depends on it because bats, with the second best hearing, love to munch moths. When night falls, your backyard becomes an aerial combat zone where listening means life...or death.

God says as much. Listening leads to life, and He offers up that advice in three key chapters from the Bible, often called God's Word, but for our auditory purposes let's call it His Voice. Psalm 19, Romans 1, and Isaiah 55 all make declarations about listening to Him to live and/or seeing His invisibility. Strangely, His attempts to reach us are silent.

Like a fluttering moth, which is a threat as we sleep (over 20 species live by landing near our eyes and jabbing a long barbed tube into them to drink our tears), His communication is as a lover's whisper uttered in two non-verbal devices — Creation (a Key West sunset detonation) and Writing (His Voice on a page). So why is God this subtle, only purring?

Well, there's a lot of static. Years ago, the deaf used a metal Ear Trumpet to hear, and were said to have a "tin ear." Spiritually, we all have a "sin ear." This condition makes us deaf, indifferent, a back turning that hears God as noise. Ironically, the physically blind and deaf know He exists by feeling the sun's heat (Psalm 19:6). Helen Keller, deaf and blind, said of Jesus, *"I always knew God was there. I just did not know his name."*

This means we can hear and not listen. See and be blind. Jesus, who invented ears, said, *"He who has ears, let him hear."* Clearly having two fleshy blobs on the side of your head doesn't mean you know how to listen. Any parent or teacher knows that. We must really want to listen, to know Him, to seek Him, and that means desperation, to be thirsty.

As a child, Helen was trapped in darkness, unable to communicate, frustrated. Her dam burst when she learned her first word, w-a-t-e-r, spelled out in her hand at a pump by her teacher who used finger spelling and palm writing. She grasped what water was as it gushed over her hand! Helen finally understood, and was freed! Helen became so thirsty to learn and to listen, that she became the first deaf/blind person to graduate from college.

Hearing is like a straw stuck in your ear that only allows a trickle. We "hear" a sunset or a clever verse, like the Golden Rule, and then stroll off unaffected. Listening is different. Listeners ponder Creation (Natural Revelation) and His Voice (Special Revelation) by the gallon and it changes them. They gulp down a starry Canadian night, wonder at its vast depth, drink it in, desperate to know Him, thirsty for His Voice (Romans 1:18-25).

Taking a sip is casual (I don't absolutely need it). Being thirsty is finding a desert well (I must have it or I'll die!), like Helen's dam bursting or a moth's escape. When you are desperate someday, and I hope you're dying of thirst very soon, Jesus offers you everlasting well water for free (John 4:14, Isaiah 55:1-3, Revelation 21:6).

It's hard to hear His Voice with a straw stuck in your ear. Why not take a slow gulp from Isaiah 55, Psalm 19, and Romans 1 and then step into the moonlight? See for yourself, and listen, especially to the quietest declaration of all in Romans 1:4. It's as raucous as a sunrise, like a trumpeted eclipse, or the bellowing Grand Canyon, *"...who was declared the Son of God with power by the resurrection from the dead.... Jesus Christ our Lord."*

Week 6:
The Joyful Alley-picker

"The Kingdom of God is like a treasure hidden in a field,
which a man found and hid; and from joy over it he goes
and sells all that he has, and buys that field
(Matthew 13:44-46)."

I think trash is cool. As a kid in Detroit we used to go alley-picking all the time. We joyfully followed our sacred creed, *"One man's trash is another man's treasure."* Why root in rubbish? Because there's always a chance, a thrill, that we'd find some treasure!

In 1991, a man spent four dollars at a flea market on an ugly picture (for the frame). He dismantled it, found an envelope, and folded inside was a *Declaration of Independence* printed by John Dunlap on July 4, 1776 (only 7 of the 25 still exist). It had wet ink smudges at the folds, but those blemishes added value as it was printed that very day.

Its value is over 8 million, but value is really what one is willing to pay (last month a banana duct-taped to a picture frame sold for 6.2 million). I guess, *"Beauty is in the eye of the banana-beholder,"* but Jesus knew a priceless work of art when He saw it, and that is people. Based on what He paid, in blood, you're a very special treasure (John 3:1-16).

In the Kingdom simile, Jesus is the man, the field is the world, and you are the treasure (or "the pearl" in verses 45-46). You may not feel like treasure, maybe even wrecked your life, but God sees a pearl; so dear He *"sells all that He has"* just to buy you back. *"For the joy set before Him He endured the cross* (Hebrews 12:2)."* You're His thrill!

Why joyfully love you, happily give up all, and die on a Roman cross with a smile? Because His opinion of you is what alley-picker's see, the true worth…not the mess. Pickers look for the Dunlap behind the ugly image. The world sees four dollars, but Jesus sees you as 8 million, and knows He can change you into a living Rembrandt, if you agree.

Agree? In Luke 19, Jesus told another story about His Kingdom, of ownership and authority, but the nobleman (Jesus) was rejected, *"We*

do not want this man to reign over us," the citizens said. Whenever something broke, my Dad would say, *"I can fix that."* Our Father in Heaven says the same, *"I can fix you."* But you have to bring what's broken to Him, let Him dismantle the frame, fix you, and reign as your King of kings.

My simile is the unwanted toys on the *Island of Misfit Toys* in *Rudolph the Red-nosed Reindeer* cartoon, except that I see it as an Easter story. What's more unwanted than a corpse? We bury them and burn them. They stink, but a tomb doesn't stink if it's empty! That's what Jesus does — He rescues us, loves us, and changes death to pearls.

The largest pearl in the world is the *Giga Pearl.* It weighs over 60 pounds. The irony is that the *Giga* looks like a big white blob, not a pearl; a beach rock we'd walk past, but that misfit blob, in the eye of the right beholder, is worth 200 million today. An ecstatic Jesus sees you as His *Giga,* except that you are even more precious (1 Peter 1:18-19).

It's simple faith (John 1:12). Admit your sin, that you've trashed your life, and let Him alley-pick you up. Just bend your knee to the risen Christmas King *"where meek souls will receive Him still, the dear Christ enters in."* Christmas means there is always a chance, and Easter means your smudges are on a *"pearl of great value"* that Jesus wants.

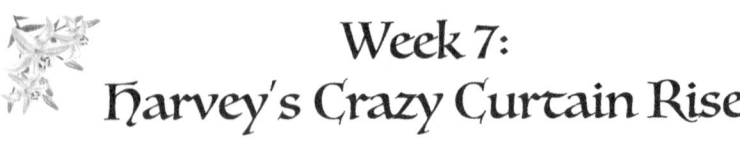

Week 7:
Harvey's Crazy Curtain Rise

"Now faith is the assurance of things hoped for, the conviction of things not seen (Hebrews 11:1)."

I keep a journal. Each morning I record my thoughts from my regular appointment with my invisible Friend, like *Harvey* in Jimmy Stewart's film by the same name (his pal is a 6'3" white rabbit). We talk. I write down my impressions. Crazy perhaps, but it's a marvelous tension, bumping the veil of the unseen realm where He lives and our world.

Today, as I opened my brand new journal (my last notebook was full), something caught my eye. On the fresh page where the ribbon bookmark had pressed into it, was a crease. I lifted the ribbon and like tracks in snow or footprints on a beach, here was a long dent that the ribbon had left behind, evidence the bookmark existed, but now entirely gone.

Today is my parent's wedding anniversary (1946). They eloped at midnight in a snowstorm and took a train from Wilkes-Barre to Baltimore. There's one record of their romantic flight. A man on the street asked if they'd like their photograph taken, and they agreed to buy one. I have that black and white image. They're gone, but it did happen.

Here's what I wrote in that new journal today (*The Faith Crease*, Ecclesiastes 12:6): *"This bookmark made an impression (on me) to prove that it was once present. The ribbon is no longer visible, but it did bodily affect the paper. The seen paper world, pinched by the unseen ribbon realm, is like Jesus' empty tomb — His burial wrappings remained, and impressed the witnesses that something happened, but Jesus was gone.*

"Like Daniel Boone reading sign — moccasin marks, broken twigs, a cold fire pit — someone was here and someone left (a mark). Gone, past tense, and yet present tense. Everything we see, a wedding photograph, a dented fender, tire treads, is assurance "it" happened. There is more than meets the eye, and a careful eye can see a "Harvey."

"It reminds me of a fine theater's heavy curtain, bumped against as the actors prepare the stage set behind it, but we in the audience can only anticipate what wonders await us. Then, the curtain stops moving; the house lights dim; an orchestra in a hidden pit strikes a note and the curtain rises! 'A conviction...of things...not seen' is alive! That's Easter!" I showed my wife this dented page (and what I wrote). She couldn't see the crease. It was faint, but if she tilted the journal in the light, it appeared out of nowhere. Obviously, Jesus is my unseen Friend. Most people don't "see" His dent on the Bible's pages, and think I'm crazy talking into thin air...as thin as my bookmark ribbon, or a sunbeam.

"I was standing today in the dark toolshed. The sun was shining outside and through the crack at the top of the door there came a sunbeam. From where I stood that beam of light, with the specks of dust floating in it, was the most striking thing in the place. Everything else was almost pitch-black. I was seeing the beam, not seeing things by it.

"Then I moved, so that the beam fell on my eyes. Instantly the whole previous picture vanished. I saw no toolshed, and (above all) no beam. Instead I saw, framed in the irregular cranny at the top of the door, green leaves moving on the branches of a tree outside and beyond that, 90 odd million miles away, the sun. Looking along the beam, and looking at the beam are very different experiences." The great C. S. Lewis saw that.

The unseen logic is endless. The acorn that you never saw is an oak in your yard. My brothers and I are in that Baltimore photo. Follow the trail all the way back, to Genesis, and there stands Jesus waiting for you to see Him. You can meet our mutual friend (Lewis was crazy too) in the Gospel of John, where He said, *"Come and you will see."*

Just open the Bible, tilt the page a bit, look past the beam, and see His crease. Lewis stepped behind the curtain in 1963. He's gone, but his words are a record that he was here. If this sounds nuts (acorns), then brace yourself. I'm naming my bookmark after Lewis. I think he'd like my ribbon-rabbit to be called...*Harvey.* I can see that logic. Can you?

Week 8:
What Does Purple Taste Like?

"For you are bringing some strange things to our ears...
(Acts 17:20)."

November 22, 1963 — Clive Staples Lewis died on the same day as John Fitzgerald Kennedy and Aldous Huxley. They've been dead almost as long as I've been alive, but for many of you they have been dead longer than you have even lived. Stop and think of that. Now ask yourself, *"Where are they exactly?"* Such important men just vanished?

All of them were important men who entered eternity on the same day; the most powerful man in the free world, a well-known British agnostic writer, and a famous Irish-born Christian writer, who profoundly said this about our leaving in *The Weight of Glory:*

"If we consider the unblushing promises of reward and the staggering nature of the rewards in the Gospels, it would seem that Our Lord finds our desires not too strong, but too weak. We are half-hearted creatures, fooling about with drink and sex and ambitions when infinite joy is offered us, like an ignorant child who wants to go on making mud pies in a slum because he cannot imagine what is meant by the offer of a holiday at the sea. We are far too easily pleased."

Another way of thinking of this offer is *"the enemy of the best is the good."* We're distracted by what we can see squish between our toes, and miss out on going away to a vast new world — content in a child's playground when flight is possible. In short, we settle. An enemy indeed, but who distracts us from slipping our muddy bonds to fly off?

The Bible says that Satan knows God, knows that He is real, has talked with Him, seen Him, defied Him, and even believes in Him. This knowledge is not a saving-eternal faith (a submission to Him as Lord and King). Such genuine faith is doing something about it. *"Even so faith, if it has no works, is dead* (James 2:17)." True trust precedes action.

Writing is like that. I can think all about writing a movie, but a scene must be put on a page (and total about 120 pages to be a script).

Anything else is Jell-O in your pocket. God is a bit like that. There is a substance to Him, but as a Spirit He doesn't stay in our pocket; He is unconfined. A hard-to-hold jiggle, and perhaps a bit like tasting a color.

We all know the color Purple, but what if I told you that it had a taste (not a grape flavor), a new other worldly sensation, strange and marvelous, like a holiday at the sea. This is what Paul presented to the Greeks in Athens...a new God flavor...strange to ears and tongues, but very much a real taste. Resurrection! Here's Paul's holiday offer...

"Therefore having overlooked the times of ignorance, God is now declaring to men that all everywhere should repent, because He has fixed a day in which He will judge the world in righteousness through a Man whom He has appointed, having furnished proof to all men by raising him from the dead."

When Gary Habermas agreed to write the Introduction for *52 Thinks About God II*, I was thrilled. He is the foremost scholar on this Purple "proof" and you can gobble it down right now on his website for free. Your ignorance about the taste of Purple is no longer an excuse on the day when we all stand with Lewis, JFK, and Huxley. Just take a lick.

Or will you stay in your slum, an ignorant child in the mud with temporary things when infinite joy is at the seashore? God is no longer overlooking your ignorance as an excuse. He has declared repentance (get up and leave your mud pies behind) and wants you to get to the beach for a staggering good time (sample Gary's lifework on savory Purple).

Now then, the next time you go to a funeral or pass a cemetery, don't ask yourself, *"Where are they exactly?"* Ask yourself this instead, *"Am I far too easily pleased?"* Or to put it in biblical terms, *"Taste and see that the Lord is good* (Psalm 34:8)." Please, act on His beach offer, by faith, and take a tiny nibble. Trust me, Gary's website is delish!

18

Week 9:
Memento Mori

"But the Lord is with me like a dread champion (Jeremiah 20:11)."

It's safe to say we've all forgotten the infamous Amy Archer-Gilligan by now, who was strangely enough born on Halloween in 1868, and her famous Hollywood adaptation few remember. Allow me to jog your memory a bit, or reap a new one for you, grim as it is.

Amy shocked the country in 1916 by pretending to be a caregiver for the elderly and then killed 48 people in her Windsor, Connecticut home, with at least five murdered by poison. The death penalty was ordered after five bodies were exhumed on site and found to be full of arsenic (she sent her own clients to buy arsenic for her at the drugstore!).

One of my top five movies of all-time was inspired by this serial killer… Frank Capra's comedy, *Arsenic and Old Lace* (Cary Grant, 1944). On his wedding day, Mortimer Brewster discovers his two sweet old spinster aunts are poisoning lonely old men with arsenic-tainted elderberry wine and buried a dozen in their basement…as a kindness!

Our fascination with Death knows no bounds. A forgotten Latin phrase comes to mind, *Memento Mori*, which means, "remember that you must die" or "remember death." How strange to "remember death" in a classic Halloween comedy film from this horror hotel, even copying into the film Amy's grisly tact of advertising in the newspaper for boarders!

Or consider the 1921 painting, *Victoria Mortis* by Owe Zerge, depicting a naked boy losing a chess game to a creepy skeletal foe. You may recognize *Mortis* in Zerge's Latin title as in "rigor mortis" (stiffness of death). Add *Victoria* and with a confident Death leaning in on the hapless teen, the intended translation is quite clear, "Victory of Death."

I prefer my favorite artist's take on Death, Winslow Homer's *The Life Line* (1884). A soggy sailor rescues a stricken woman from a storm, cradled safely in his arms on a breeches buoy cable from her ship. *Lifesavers* were real heroes, now also forgotten, and the precursor of our *Coast Guard* (picture a basket hoisting that woman into a helicopter).

The *Lifesavers* (on coast guard duty from 1872 to 1915) had a biblical motto, *"You have to go, but you don't have to come back."* That rings of Christmas ("I have to go to rescue them") and Good Friday ("but I'll die in the attempt."). Ah, but imagine the surprised look on Death's face when God's mystery was revealed on Easter morn! *"If they would have understood it, they would not have crucified the Lord of glory* (1 Corinthians 2:8)."

If I painted Death it would have two panels, a bloody, unrecognizable Jesus playing chess with a smug, arms folded Death, and the nude boy cowering behind Him in abject fear. The next panel would be Jesus aglow as his risen dread champion, and the boy pointing with glee at the chessboard. The title would be *Novissime Moventur,* "The Last Move."

Like the *Lifesavers,* Winslow, and Amy Archer-Gilligan, Johnny Hart is mostly forgotten today too. He was a popular comic strip artist (think Charles M. Schulz and *Peanuts*), with his *B.C.* strip about cavemen, and a real treat in our Sunday newspaper. My favorite *B.C.* comic strip had only three panels to convey Hart's genius.

In the first panel a thoughtful caveman is seated, staring off into the distance, and says, *"I hate the term 'Good Friday.'"* His fellow caveman is puzzled, and asks, *"Why?"*

In the next scene the forlorn caveman replies, *"My Lord was hanged on a tree."* His buddy asks a second question. *"If you were going to be hanged on that day, and He volunteered to take your place, how would you feel?"*

Still sad in the last panel, he manages only a single glum word. *"Good."* The other caveman walks off and with Johnny's clever insight says, *"Have a nice day."*

Should we remember Death, be aware of our mortality in paint, film, and cartoons? I think so, but not as a morbid victor, but as God's mystery move that was eventually and eternally "good" for us. Rolling away His stone was a checkmate Satan never saw coming! And so, I say to you, I hope you have a very Good Friday remembering that!

Week 10:
Ivan, Origins, and the Great Taboo

"Truly, Thou art a God who hides Himself, O God of Israel, Savior (Isaiah 45:15)!"

"Nothing is certain except death and taxes." We've all quoted it, but most don't know Ben Franklin said it, or that half of us don't even pay our taxes (about 700 billion last year). We complain about taxes, but they're not at all certain. This brings us to Ivan.

You've recited Ivan Krylov's words too, probably 200 times. They relate to the one and only certainty, death, or in Ivan's words, *"the elephant in the room."* This solo trip, our grave guarantee, is mostly ignored. We hide from death, shield ourselves from cadavers, graveyards, and funeral homes (only 25 percent of us have pre-paid our own funeral).

Even now, you're tempted to stop reading — the *Grim Reaper* is a drag, our dozing elephant in the room that we tiptoe past. Death is "taboo," a word most don't know the origin of (Captain Cook first heard it in 1777 in Tonga, then called the Friendly Islands).

It's ironic, since our life is so fragile, a wispy spider's thread that can snap in a breeze. King Solomon called it *"the silver cord"* and to *"remember God before it is broken* (Ecclesiastes 12:6).*"* As children, we rarely even considered death, but it always twisted silently overhead, an unknown reality that our parents kept hidden away in the shadows.

In my Detroit neighborhood, when the streetlights came on it meant I had to go home to get up for school the next day. Like death, this rule was not negotiable in our house. But in the summertime, all bets were off and darkness meant more time to play our favorite game…Hide and Seek Tag! Being "It" was a big deal and the honor chosen carefully.

We'd put one foot in a circle and someone tapped our toes as he said, *"Eeny, meeny, miny, moe catch an elephant by his toe, if he hollers, let him go, eeny, meeny, miny, moe."* That last moe got dismissed; he'd start again, until only one was left to be "It."

Whoever was "It" had to find the hidden kids after counting to 20 on the front porch, but he also had to protect that porch (we called it "Gool," a variation of Goal, a safe spot). So the farther away he got from Gool in his search for us, the better our chance to race to the porch and not get tagged out. If successful, we'd shout, *"Ollie, Ollie, oxen free!"*

Those kid memories are precious to me, but where did those crazy phrases come from — Ollie, Ollie, oxen free, Eeny, meeny, miny, moe, and Gool? They're as mysterious as Tonga, Krylov...and God, who said that He hides Himself. Why does God hide, and seem so far off? Or is it something else entirely, something that has to do with...us?

I think I know the answer. Do you? God hints at it in Isaiah 55:6, *"Seek the Lord while He may be found. Call upon him while He is near."* God does hide, but He's close, and can be found. Isaiah's next verse, verse 7, has the answer (and how to toss our elephant out of the room). Now, you're "It." Go, and seek. Find the Hidden One (Acts 17:27).

22

Week 11:
The Milk Jug Fix

"He has fixed...a day (Acts 17:31)."

"A movie is something that gives the illusion of stopping time," says Bob Dylan. *"It's all happening in your brain and it seems like nothing else is going on in the world. Time has stopped. The world could be coming to an end outside, but for you time has stopped."* Eventually, however, the screen credits will roll. The "fix" is definitely in. It all ends.

Two famous people "expired" recently and it stopped me cold. (Insert your own loss-shock here because the point isn't their fame, but that time stopped for them on a specific day.) This was no movie. They died. We prefer not to think about our own day, but if you don't consider *"the certainty of death,"* as Gimli the Dwarf says in *The Lord of the Rings* film, I submit that you're living in a movie theater — a dark illusion.

King David wondered about his last day too. In Psalm 42 he wrote, *"When shall I come and appear before God?"* This got me thinking... what is my day to *"appear?"* Is it a Monday? Spring? What if it ruins Christmas Day for my family? Or is it close, like a *Twilight Zone* episode that matches the date on the gallon of milk in my refrigerator?

In the Book of Acts, chapter 17, the Apostle Paul says that God has fixed a day when *"for you time has stopped."* Paul went to Athens to their famous Aeropagus Theater and challenged the great Greek thinkers about *"Jesus and the resurrection."* The *"very religious,"* Paul calls them, and he *"reasoned with them every day."* Here's the gist:

- God knows everyone's mystery date, having *"determined their appointed times."*

- Our milk jug certainty means we're in a fix, so we *"should seek God."* Why?

- Because He's *"not far from each of us,"* and can help erase our expiration date. How?

23

- Jesus is alive, so God is *"now declaring to men that all everywhere should repent."*

God has commanded your repentance (to change your mind) about the back-from-the-dead Jesus and to submit to Him as your King. We bristle at being told what to do, but He has that right since He fixed our death problem (Romans 6:23). Our recoil confirms our rebellion, but He's not being ruthless. It's a declaration of love, to help, to stop our screen credits from rolling, but we're so twisted by sin we see it as bossing us around.

"He has fixed a day in which He will judge the world in righteousness through a Man whom He has appointed, having furnished proof to all men by raising Him from the dead (Acts 17:31)." His judgment is not based on your good works (Ephesians 2:8-9). It's based on our sin and our response to what Jesus did for us on the cross (Titus 3:3-7).

Paul's blast of light into Athens' darkness had two results — *"some sneered"* and *"some believed."* That's your choice too. Gimli's full quote is an appeal to his friends to be brave, to change their minds (repent), and follow him into battle, *"Certainty of death. Small chance of success. What are we waiting for?"* You don't have to follow God's command. Love is a choice, but I'd ask Gimli's question another way, *"Got milk?"*

Week 12:
Our Ancient Family Feud

"Your name will no longer be Jacob, but Israel (Genesis 32:28)."

"What's in a name?" lamented Shakespeare's Juliet Capulet, regarding her family's feud with Romeo Montague's kin. *"That which we call a rose by any other name would smell as sweet."* Romeo was her true love. It all smelled the same to her whatever his label. She didn't care if his family changed their name to Finkelstein. He was always her man.

Hollywood studios often changed actor's real names (John Wayne, Marilyn Monroe, Cary Grant, Fred Astaire, Judy Garland, and Tony Curtis come to mind). One movie star, Issur "Izzy" Danielovitch, changed his name on his own and made over 90 films. He was worth 60 million dollars when he died, but he was always just plain Izzy to his family.

Another Hollywood name-switch was in *Dances with Wolves* (inspired by true events and a kidnapped white child, Cynthia Parker, who was raised as *"Stands With A Fist"*). In telling Kevin Costner her Sioux name, she stands up hard, defiant, to convey her new name/identity. That name/identity connection could also be said of Blaise Pascal, the French genius who "torched" the Math world (except that Blaise means "to lisp").

Lisping or not, Pascal said, *"All men seek happiness. This is the motive of every action of every man, even of those who hang themselves."* It's true. We are all about self. In any photo we always look for ourselves first (not to mention our Selfie pics). We all chase our own self-interests to be happy, to be on the throne, and to have it our own way.

The Bible agrees. *"All of us like sheep have gone astray, each of us has turned to his own way* (Isaiah 53:6)." But this astray-way is an empty road; such selfishness poisons the soul (Romans 6:23). No matter what you've done, He promises if you give up, return to Him, you'll find compassion, an abundant pardon, peace, and joy (Isaiah 55:1-12).

Pascal also said, *"What else does this craving, and this helplessness, proclaim but that there was once in man a true happiness, of which all*

that now remains is the empty print and trace? This he tries in vain to fill with everything around him, seeking in things that are not there the help he cannot find in those that are, though none can help, since this infinite abyss can be filled only with an infinite and immutable object; in other words by God Himself." If you want true happiness, something has to change your name/identity.

One famous name switch occurred when God changed Jacob to Israel (Issur in Yiddish, Kirk Douglas' first name). Jacob's name/identity meant *"one who takes control,"* but a meeting with a pre-incarnate Jesus who wrestled Jacob into submission, broke him and his pride. His new "say Uncle" moniker, Israel, means *"one who clings to God,"* not self.

We're all wrestling with God, and it's an ancient family feud (Colossians 2:13-14). Our sin has us at odds with Him, in a headlock, and we must yield to Him to be free, or our "name" will always have a Jacob stench of self and death. Only Jesus can give us a new name/identity (Revelation 2:17) because of His sin sacrifice (Hebrews 10:14-18).

Kirk Douglas once said, *"Making a movie is like dancing in wet cement."* That sounds like wrestling. A life astray, defiant, standing with a fist, without Jesus, is exactly that. Juliet sees her struggle for happiness is in Romeo's last name, and her problem speaks to us too. *"'Tis but thy name that is my enemy; thou art thyself ...O, be some other name!"*

We all need Jesus to give us a new name/identity (John 3:3). Indeed, submit and let God prevail in your life. Be an Izzy, a God-gripper. O, be some other name. Cry Uncle!

Week 13:
George Jingles and the Naked Spuds

"For we have brought nothing into the world, so we cannot take anything out of it either (1 Timothy 6:7)."

"For over a thousand years Roman conquerors returning from the wars enjoyed the honor of triumph, a tumultuous parade. In the procession came trumpeters, musicians and strange animals from conquered territories, together with carts laden with treasure and captured armaments. The conqueror rode in a triumphal chariot, the dazed prisoners walking in chains before him. Sometimes his children robed in white stood with him in the chariot or rode the trace horses. A slave stood behind the conqueror holding a golden crown, and whispering in his ear a warning: that all glory is fleeting."

George C. Scott spoke those lines over 50 years ago in the film *"Patton."* His last four words stab us — all glory is fleeting. They stabbed him too. Almost no one remembers that he won the Oscar for playing General Patton ("Old Blood and Guts"), or that he was the first actor to refuse it. At the 43rd Academy Awards there was "No Guts, No Glory."

I witnessed glory 40 years ago today, on October 14th, when my Detroit Tigers won the *World Series* (my ticket was a measly $15), but alas… *tempus fugit*, a Roman's jingle from 29 B.C. that in Latin means *"time flies."* Sadly, I saw one of my '84 Tigers last week, now in a wheelchair, debilitated by strokes and disease. Patton's jingle again.

The Apostle Paul nailed both jingles together. *"For we have brought nothing into the world, and so we cannot take anything out of it either."* Today we'd say there's no U-Haul hitch on a hearse. Colonel *"finger-lickin' good"* Sanders quipped, *"No use being the richest man in the cemetery because you can't do any business in there."* True dat.

But not all that jingles is true (we call that advertising). A *McDonald's* semi-truck recently assaulted me with two gigantic Idaho potatoes under the phrase *"Destined For Greatness."* I laughed out loud!

Skinned alive, sliced up, drowned in boiling oil, and eaten by a stranger...that's greatness? Their final destiny is far less noble, that's for sure.

But what is sure, what's true? As a boy, my Mother often asked me, *"What do you know for sure?"* Sure things are *"as scarce as hen's teeth"* now, but the Bible says that you can be certain of this truth...you can know for sure you're going to Heaven. Are you 100 percent positive you'll get in? You can be. That's precisely why the Bible was written.

"He who has the Son has the life; he who does not have the Son of God does not have the life. These things I have written to you who believe in the name of the Son of God, in order that you may know that you have eternal life (1 John 5:12-13).*"* You're either spiritually alive or spiritually dead, and no one has the Son automatically (Ephesians 2:1).

You have to choose to receive Him (John 1:12) by asking Jesus to literally enter into your body (Colossians 1:27), and then His Spirit will make you alive (John 3:1-21). It's a total surrender, but unlike Patton's story, the chained prisoners become the white robed children of the One with the golden crown (1 Corinthians 15:50-56). *"Has the Son"* is not a silly jingle like some use to sell French fries. *"Has the Son"* is a promise from God.

28

Week 14:
"But What Does It All Mean?"

"Time is running backwards and so is the Bride (Bob Dylan)."

What does R.S.V.P. stand for? We all think we know what it means, but most of us can't explain it. We typically see it on a wedding invitation, which I confess has less allure for me as I age. But I do look forward to the wedding toast-speeches. Everyone loves a good story, especially if it's true. Jesus knew that, and so did the great C. S. Lewis.

In Lewis' first *Chronicles of Narnia* book, Aslan, the lion King of Narnia, is murdered by the Witch and then rises again. A shocked Susan Pevensie asks him, *"But what does it all mean?"* Aslan answers her, and also our ancient question about the meaning of life:

"If she (the Witch) could have looked a little further back, into the stillness and darkness before Time dawned, she would have read there a different incantation. She would have known that when a willing victim who had committed no treachery was killed in a traitor's stead, the Table would crack and Death itself would start working backward."

Imagine God as the Captain on an old ship and He issues a command, *"Full Reverse!"* The Pilot on the Bridge then throws the lever on the Engine Order Telegraph — that circular device with a lever that rings a bell when pushed or pulled to inform the Engine Room of direction and speed, as we saw in the James Cameron film *Titanic* (1997).

After His resurrection, Time reversed, as Bob Dylan sings in *Ring Them Bells*, and so is the Bride of Christ (the Church). The *Table of Time* cracked, and everything is now Full Astern — back to Eden, back to Paradise, back to our Creator. You don't have to climb the Himalayas to ask a wise man what's the meaning of life. In a word, Easter!

If you still wonder like Susan, then I suggest a wander...through Lewis' *Narnia* series (a fast 19 hour read). Lewis did a grand job expanding on Aslan's answer in these children stories for adults that reveal the Bible's

main message — immortality! Lewis was very adept at it, but the true wedding toast Master, who existed before Time dawned, is Jesus.

My favorite Jesus "toast" is in Luke chapter 15, and it begins with, *"A certain man had two sons."* It's all about going backward, like a bell's clapper that rings back and forth. Two sons. Two choices. Two directions. Turning around. An eyewitness of the bodily resurrection, John the Apostle, knew firsthand about turning back and what it all means:

"He who has the Son, has the life; he who does not have the Son of God, does not have the life. These things I have written to you who believe in the name of the Son of God, in order that you may know that you have eternal life (1 John 5:12-13)." In a word, Easter!

That's why the Bible was written, so that you can know for sure you're going to Heaven. It's no mountaintop mystery. God says there are two kinds of people, those who have the Son inside of their body (because they asked Him to come inside, Ephesians 1:13-14), and those who are empty inside and do not have the Son. That brings us back to R.S.V.P.

R.S.V.P. is an old French phrase *(Répondez s'il vous plait)* initialized into, *"Respond if you please."* In Matthew 22, Jesus made another toast about a King giving a wedding reception for his son. The invitations went out, but the guests made excuses. I'm too busy, I don't care, and some even got angry. In a word, get lost. Their E.O.T. lever was in neutral, straight up, ignoring the Easter Captain. They had no time for it.

Each wedding has a date, a time limit, except in God's hourglass the sand trickles up, backward. We all think we know…what Easter means, but we don't know, not really, not unless we R.S.V.P. If you do respond, then you truly know (that you have eternal life). Please, say you'll come. That is what it's all about, Susan. Easter is an invitation.

Week 15:
The Holy Hollow

"And I saw the dead, the great and the small, standing before the throne, and books were opened; and another book was opened, which is the book of life (Revelation 20:11-15)."

A taxi driver and a preacher arrive at the Pearly Gates. Peter asks the driver a question, nods, gives him a gold harp, and in he goes. The preacher gets a rusty harp and is told to wait. Hours later, the preacher demands an explanation. Peter says, *"It's based on merit. Your sermons put folks to sleep, but when he was driving...people prayed up a storm!"*

If Peter's only entry question was how many dumb Pearly Gates jokes exist, I think we'd all flunk. I tried to find out, but no luck (there's too many, which is ironic since we think entry is based on luck, or merit). That's the real joke; it's neither. The worst "sex, drugs, and rock-and-roll" felon can be sure of going to Heaven — today — before they die.

This is why the Bible was written, getting into Heaven is not a guessing game. *"These things I have written to you who believe in the name of the Son of God, in order that you may know that you have eternal life (1 John 5:13)."* You can know with 100% certainty that when you die, you'll get in. Death is definite, but arriving in Heaven can be assured.

Regarding "arriving," *Led Zeppelin's* lead singer, Robert Plant, said, *"To have money at last, is just another figure in my mind of mass acceptance which is what we all work for; I mean everybody, however how much they like to deny the fact, really wants in the end to be accepted."* Pretty keen insight for a 22-year old rocker, as is this *NFL* star at 27...

A. J. Brown just won the *Super Bowl.* After global adulation he said, *"It didn't do anything for me."* This famous millionaire athlete realized that an *NFL* championship didn't fill his heart's divot. Apologies to Robert Plant, but "the hole remains the same." In Mere Christianity, C. S. Lewis cut deeper into our cardiac cavity with these words:

"Most people, if they had really learned to look into their own hearts, would know that they do want, and want acutely, something that cannot be had in this world. There are all sorts of things in this world that offer to give it to you, but they never quite keep their promise. If I find in myself a desire which no experience in this world can satisfy, the most probable explanation is that I was made for another world (with Pearly Gates)."

Peter knew this, that we were made to be with God, and that all the Pearly Gates jokes are a joke, and it's on us. Peter isn't asking questions; he's giving an answer. Peter wrote, *"You shall be holy for I am holy (1 Peter 1:16)."* Be holy? Perfect? That's impossible! If that's God's standard, then no one gets in because nobody's perfect (Matthew 5:48).

Exactly! And more importantly, we can't make ourselves holy. *"If righteousness comes through the Law, then Christ died needlessly (Galatians 2:21)."* If we can be acceptable to God by keeping the Law (doing good deeds), then why did Jesus die? That's the real Pearly Gates question — *"If it's all based on our merit, then why did Jesus have to die?"*

This is a heavy question. If we think our acceptance with God is on our own merit; that being "good enough" is the answer we think Peter requires at the Gate; that our good deeds will be weighed out on God's giant scale against our sin to prove that we're not that bad, then why did Jesus have to die? This "we think" is not in the Bible (Titus 3:5).

So here's my Pearly Gates question…when Jesus was dying on the cross, He promised one of the thieves crucified with Him that he would be in Paradise that very day (Luke 23:43), so how did this thief become holy if he literally couldn't do anything? That answer — what filled his holy hollow — is what's coming up next in our Part II.

Week 16:
The Holy Hollow II

"But with precious blood, as of a lamb unblemished and spotless, the blood of Christ (1 Peter 1:19)."

In the first Holy Hollow column we established that our soul longs to be accepted and fulfilled, but the answer is only found in another world where God reigns. Our entry there requires what we don't have and can't make, God's essence — Holiness. Peter's Pearly Gates answer is bad news..."*You must be holy for I am holy* (1 Peter 1:16)."

Now holiness may sound like a bad haircut in a short-sleeved polyester shirt with a clip-on tie, and definitely not *Led Zeppelin* cool, but God says holiness is not only cool, it's the only key to open the Pearly Gates. And, since we all flunk out because nobody's perfect, it also seems like a cruel joke. What gives? Is God a tyrant playing games?

This may help. Imagine your soul is a big red balloon. How many pins do you have to stick in it to make it a blobby, lifeless mess on the ground? One or a thousand, it doesn't matter because perfection has been ruined. All the oxygen (holiness) is gone. Nothing you can do will restore its perfection. You're pricked, helpless, and fall from the sky.

"For whoever keeps the whole law and yet stumbles in one point, he has become guilty of all (James 2:10)." If sin is a needle, whether it's one or a thousand jabs, holiness is lost forever. It's not the quality or quantity of the sin, per se. It's the absence of perfection. *"For all have sinned and fall short of the glory of God* (Romans 3:23)." We all fall short.

Your crash is so hard that it cracks open a mile wide chasm. On the other side is hope, the distant *Land of Oxygen!* How can you get over the canyon that you made to get what you need to float again? You can't. You're nailed to the ground, like the thief on the cross, doomed, unless help comes. Would the *King of Oxygen* cross the chasm to help?

"But your iniquities have made a separation between you and your God, and your sins have hidden His face from you so that He does not hear (Isaiah 59:2)." "For all of us have become like one who is unclean,

and all our righteous deeds are like a filthy garment (Isaiah 64:6)." We are separated and nothing we can do will bridge that gap.

But the King did come, and with *"the spotless blood of Christ"* made a holy glue to seal our holes, then breathed life-giving oxygen into us —— God's Spirit comes inside of our body, *"You were sealed in Him with the Holy Spirit of promise* (Ephesians 1:13-14)." We are no longer empty, shriveled up blobs at the canyon's edge. His mercy saves us.

The balloon can do nothing, but ask for help and then accept it, what the Bible calls grace. You must accept grace. But this is very hard because you have to admit you have an ugly hole that you can't fix, and only the *Balloon Maker* can repair and re-inflate you. It takes humility to accept grace, to give up, so that He can smear you with His holy glue.

Paul said this in Ephesians 2:8-9, *"For by grace you have been saved through faith; and that not of yourselves, it is the gift of God; not as result of works, that no one should boast."* It is this simple: ask Him to help, to save you, and receive Him (John 1:12). This genuine contrition and faith makes you holy. Look at my favorite New Testament verse:

"He made Him who knew no sin to be sin on our behalf, that we might become the righteousness of God in Him (2 Corinthians 5:21)." God made Jesus, the Holy One, to be sin on our behalf, so that we could be as holy as God Himself...in Him, in Jesus. Problem solved! Balloons inflate and soar over the chasm to Paradise (2 Peter 3:13).

So what did the thief do? Nothing. In genuine faith, he asked Jesus to save him by His blood sacrifice, the Passover Lamb, *"who takes away the sins of the world."* He simply gave up and accepted grace. It's so easy, and yet so hard, to be humble and ask to be rescued. But to think we're good enough, or did enough, is the real Pearly Gates joke.

Week 17:
Compared to a Bowl of Rice

"Behold, I have inscribed you on the palms of My hands...
(Isaiah 49:16)."

"Twice a day," the reporter wept into the camera, *"this African woman gets a tiny bowl of rice for her, and her child to live on."* He composed himself. *"You may not think you're rich (enough to help), but compared to this poor woman, you are wildly wealthy."*

Compared to the *USC* football player who just died –– a *Heisman Trophy* runner-up, who led the nation in rushing yards in 1967 and 1968, the first pick in the *AFL Draft*, an *NFL Hall of Famer*, a movie star, and *NBC* sports announcer, we all fall short and seem poor. But his wealth and success were all undone by one question, *"Is O.J. Simpson guilty?"*

The country was divided on whether or not he murdered his wife Nicole Brown Simpson and Ron Goldman. He was acquitted in the famous 1995 trial, but then found liable in a 1997 civil trial owing both families 33.5 million. Was he guilty? We may never know, but it seems legally the answer was no, and then yes (hardly a definitive judgment).

But the Bible has a clear verdict for all of us. *"For all have sinned and fall short of the glory of God* (Romans 3:23)."* Imagine meeting someone new and you say, *"Pleased to meet you, I'm Gil. Gil Tee."* Absurd because we think we're not guilty. *"I'm good enough. My good deeds outweigh my bad deeds. Compared to Hitler, I'm not so bad."*

That's the bowl of rice problem. It all depends on what you're comparing *"it"* to. Compared to her bowl of rice, we're rich. Compared to Simpson, we're poor. Compared to Hitler, we're not guilty. But is our perception of ourselves right (I'm not that bad) and our view of God's justice correct (He loves me because after all, I'm mostly good)?

The standard God uses is Himself...holiness, perfection. *"Therefore, you are to be perfect, as your heavenly Father is perfect* (Matthew 5:48)."* Jesus Christ is "it." The sinless man, God-in-the-flesh, and

compared to Him, *"we all fall short of the glory of God."* *"There is none righteous, not even one* (Romans 3:10)." That seems awful severe.

We think God weighs out our deeds on a cosmic scale and we're obviously good enough. But there are no scales. *"For whoever keeps the whole Law and yet stumbles in one point, he has become guilty of all* (James 2:10)." *"But I did my best. Nobody's perfect. Where's the 'God is love' stuff?"* That's where the cross fits in...like a bloody glove.

Imagine if Ron Goldman's Dad took Simpson's place –– that's what God did for you! *"He made Him (Jesus) who knew no sin to be sin on our behalf, that we might become the righteousness of God in Him* (2 Corinthians 5:21)." The sinless Man reconciled God's perfect justice and His love by taking our place, and the punishment for our sins.

So now when you meet Jesus, if you are *"in Him"* and not in your unpaid sins, you can say, *"Hi, I'm 'the righteousness of God' because of Your blood. Rice to meet You."*

Week 18:
Die Rich

"For what does it profit a man to gain the whole world and forfeit his soul (Mark 8:36)?"

"I can't control getting old, but I can control getting fat." This is what I told the woman at our new gym that toured me around the facility. Her co-worker said, *"Hey! That's good! I'm putting that on our Facebook page."* So began my costly gym membership.

When your age (62) passes your birth year ('61), it's time to take the long-view. Most Americans set January goals, and the vast majority of them involve their body and their finances, which can be condensed — Die Rich. That's crass, and we may not say it out loud, but that's the gist on Monday morning. Live as long and as well as you can, right?

Spin that however you like, but it's probably true for you as well. Delay death and aging, and make as much money as you can to enjoy life...now. But what did the Son of David say about this *"now"* retirement strategy? Jesus said it's shortsighted; even if you get everything you want, your true treasure, your soul, is in jeopardy if you die in your sins.

Consider *"The Rip Van Winkle Caper,"* a favorite *Twilight Zone* episode. A scientist named Farwell steals $1 million dollars in gold with three accomplices, and with his skill they enter suspended animation for 100 years in a desert cave, hoping to wake up safe and rich. Things go awry upon waking; greed and murder take them all out but Farwell.

He dies at the end too, in the desert, offering his last gold bar to a passing stranger to save him. The man returns to his wife in their futuristic car to explain the tramp's delirium. *"Can you imagine that? He offered this to me as if it was really worth something."* He tosses the gold bar away into the hot sand, promising to send the police back for his body.

"Wasn't it worth something once?" she asks. *"Didn't people use gold for money?"*

"Sure, about 100 years or so ago...before they found a way of manufacturing it," he says.

Our thieves woke up to a world with a whole different value system. Put another way, in 100 years, what will matter most to you? Here's a hint...in Heaven they use gold for asphalt. The answer to what is truly *"precious"* and *"imperishable"* will take you a little gold digging. It's in the Apostle Peter's first letter, chapter one (1 Peter 1:3-5 and 17-19).

Rod Serling wraps up the 1961 TV lesson with black and white biblical wisdom: *"The last of four Rip Van Winkles, who all died precisely the way they lived, chasing an idol across the sand to wind up bleached dry in the hot sun as so much flotsam, worthless as the gold bullion they built a shrine to."* They foolishly chased a counterfeit security.

Security here...now, is a fallacy; death comes and riches stay. We can die rich, poor, or forgiven, but we all die. You can't control the leaving, but you can control a secure arrival. So please, take the long-view and join His gym. It's free today (Romans 6:23).

Week 19:
It's About Time...Isn't It?

"Therefore be careful how you walk, not as unwise men, but as wise, making the most of your time, because the days are evil (Ephesians 5:15-16)."

On April 18, 1955, a man who understood Time better than anyone, with perhaps the most dazzling intellect ever, could not stop Time's steady advance and got swallowed up by it. That man was Albert Einstein, the father of Quantum Physics.

Einstein figured out the space-time continuum that led to the Atomic Age, won the *Nobel Prize*, and laid the cornerstone for modern science. Despite his renown, Albert literally (and theoretically) proved that Time waits for no man, something we're forced to admit every New Year's Eve. There is an end coming.

I guess it's necessary to recognize Time each January, but I've never understood making resolutions. Lose weight. Stop smoking. Start exercising. Why? If we're honest, and take the 100-year viewpoint, resolutions to help us live longer, look better, or improve ourselves are all futile attempts to beat Time and its ravages. We need to conquer Death, not delay it, but that's impossible, right?

Well, there's another man with an even more dazzling intellect than Einstein, who was the first to actually swallow up both Time and Death. In his letter to the Colossians, the Apostle Paul called Jesus *"the invisible God"* and *"the firstborn from the dead,"*

"He is the image of the invisible God, the first-born of all creation. For by Him all things were created, both in the heavens and on earth, visible and invisible, whether thrones or dominions or rulers or authorities— all things have been created by Him and for Him. And He is before all things, and in Him all things hold together. He is also head of the body, the church; and He is the beginning, the first-born from the dead; so that He Himself might come to have first place in everything. For it was the Father's good pleasure for all the fullness to dwell in Him, and through

Him to reconcile all things to Himself, having made peace through the blood of His cross...."

The mirror proves we're all losing the race with Time. Resolutions are only a stop-gap measure. You can lose weight, but Time will still swallow you up too. Isn't it wiser to make the most of your time by investigating the claims of the only man who conquered Death? Maybe resolve this upcoming year to read just one of the four Gospels.

In 2016, I went to Israel on a 2-week writing assignment that required a hundred decisions – flights, expenses, tour guides, hotels, passports, and restaurants. It took weeks of planning. That was a trip I *"hoped"* to take, but you have a definite April 18th trip that Time silently screams in your ear every New Year's Eve. An end is coming.

How ironic to ignore that warning and just hope your permanent departure ends with a reservation. If Jesus is alive, perhaps your resolution should be to make peace with Him and give Jesus *"first place in everything."* After all, it's about Time…isn't it?

Week 20:
For God So Doved the World

"Outside of a dog, a book is man's best friend.
Inside of a dog, it's too dark to read." – Groucho Marx

I own more books than I have years left to read. A hefty chore for my kids someday, but my favorite will be easy to lift at a mere 1,082 words. And yet, the depth of those 48 verses makes the *Mariana Trench*, at 36,000 feet below sea level, just a muddy ditch.

When Jesus was challenged for proof that He was the Anointed One — the eternal Son of King David, predicted all over the Scriptures as the God-Man who would restore Israel and bless the nations — He said one sign would be given...the Dove sign (Matthew 12).

Children know the story from Sunday school...a rebel refuses to obey God, spends three nights in a Sea Monster's belly (where it's too dark to read), and gets puked onto dry land for a second chance. It sums up the Old Testament message, sort of God's *Grand Canyon* equivalent, impressive alone, but up close, toes on the edge, the sheer scope overwhelms.

In Hebrew, Jonah means *"dove,"* a sin sacrifice that the poor offered at the Jerusalem Temple. His Father's name means *"truth,"* so Jonah is the Son of Truth, a sacrifice. When the storm rages, he tells the pagan sailors of his sin and to toss him into the sea to save themselves, but they are afraid that his *"innocent blood"* would be on their hands. Finally, they relent and over he goes. The storm stops and the big lesson truly begins.

Penned over 750 years before Jesus, Jonah is a satire where everything is upside down, even Jonah himself is an inverted type of Jesus, but the story's clever construction proves it's God's Word. The most obvious miracle is what Jesus says in Matthew 12, *"For just as Jonah was three days and three nights in the belly of the Sea Monster so shall the Son of Man be three days and three nights in the heart of the earth."* The Messiah will...die!

Jonah sums up God's love in the Old Testament, and John 3:16 sums it up in the New Testament (that poster you often see at sporting events — John 3:16, which means the Gospel of John, chapter 3, verse 16 — *"For God so loved the world that He gave His only begotten Son, that whoever believes in Him should not perish, but have eternal life."*). This resurrection Dove sign proved His deity, confirmed His death paid for the world's sins (Isaiah 53), and God's unfathomable love (Jonah 4:2 and Romans 5:8).

I can't plumb all the depths of Jonah here, but you can…through a free class on Jonah offered by *The Bible Project*, (you may be familiar with their impressive animated summaries of the Bible's 66 books). Go to bibleproject.com and their classroom offerings. If the Bible is new to you or you want to dive deeper, you'll be amazed by their fine work on God's miraculous Book that is truly your best friend, because it will light up your darkness, even if you're a rebel in a Sea Monster's belly (Psalm 119:105)!

Week 21:
Chief Stone

"Unless a grain of wheat falls into the earth and dies...
(John 12:24)."

The Red Balloon won an Oscar for Albert Lamorisse in 1956 with a
simple story — a magical balloon befriends a lonely French boy on his
way to school. I saw it at *Leslie Elementary* at about the same age as the
film's star — Albert's five-year-old son, Pascal.

For 34 minutes, and with almost no words, his enchanting spell took
me to Paris to see an over-sized ruby red balloon pal along with Pascal
through his harsh, drab-gray streets.

I watched it today and was instantly back in that dark *Leslie* auditorium,
convinced again that his balloon was alive! Perfectly round, that vibrant
candy apple orb also reminded me of something else that's living...
God's Word. The Bible is a perfect reflection of God's holiness and His
love, but it's also a spiritual thermometer that shows us how sick we are.

"For all have sinned and fall short of the glory of God (Romans 3:23)."
We've all broken at least one of the Ten Commandments. (Not you?
Well, you just did!). So how many pins do you have to stick in a balloon
before you break its perfection?

Albert shows the answer and our sinfulness when a mob of children
throw stones at Pascal's sentient friend. When just one stone hits the
balloon, it falls to the earth and dies. One pin, one sin, or one stone and
perfection dies. *"For whoever keeps the whole Law and yet stumbles in
one point, he has become guilty of all* (James 2:10)."

We're all in that stone-throwing mob, guilty and dead. *"For the
wages of sin is death* (Romans 6:23)." Thankfully God hurled a stone
too. The target was sin and death. His aim and stone were perfect...
Jesus Christ. Psalm 118 and Matthew 21 tell us that Jesus became God's
chief cornerstone (the first stone laid by a mason, a reference point for
all the other stones to be perfect). The Perfect came to make us holy
(2 Corinthians 5:21).

Sadly for Albert, life imitated art when he was 48 years old. While filming a documentary over a dam in Iran Albert's helicopter got tangled in some power lines. Pascal was onboard and miraculously leapt from the helicopter. He survived the crash that killed the pilot and his Father. Great or small, young or old, because of sin death is a real threat, especially if we die in our sins. Fortunately, his film had a better ending.

Balloons from all over Paris escape their tethers and rush to a heartbroken Pascal. Mobbed by the colorful blob, he grabs their strings and they lift him up and over the city in a wonderful resurrection moment. Apparently, his friend sent help…just like God did when the chief cornerstone was laid down in the grave for our sin and then rose again.

Our sin murdered Jesus just as sure as that stone killed Pascal's floating friend. Our stone broke that union with God, but Jesus came to restore us…if we grab His tether. John chapter 12 says He can lift you up too. Let Him lift you up this Easter, over your drab-gray grave, and surrender to Him as your Master, your Lord, and your Chief Stone.

Week 22:
The Sick Sense

"...but the things which are not seen are eternal (2 Corinthians 4:18)."

I love surprise endings, like *The Sixth Sense* film — Dr Crowe tries to cure young Cole's neurosis (he sees the unseen world, ghosts), but the trick isn't revealed until the very end, when Crowe realizes his gunshot wound in the opening scene was fatal; that's why Cole, *"I see dead people,"* can see him. Dr Crowe has been dead...the whole movie! Tricked!

Like Dr Crowe, we're unaware that we are dead too, spiritually speaking, and the unseen world is the actual reality. The Bible reveals the trick in Ephesians 2:1, *"You were dead in your trespasses and sins."* But the Sin-trick is still in play and Sin needs removal before our physical demise seals our fate (John 8:24).

Like thick scales on the eyes of our heart, we've all been duped. *"The heart is more deceitful than all else and is desperately sick* (Jeremiah 17:9).*"* We think this is really living, but we're actually dead zombies. Sounds like a real *Matrix* movie, eh? Deceived means you don't know you're deluded.

Even now you question this very point, that you're Sin-tricked; unconcerned, trusting in your five senses. I can prove it to you, but I can't convince you. Jesus said as much, *"If they will not listen to Moses and the Prophets, neither will they be persuaded if someone rises from the dead (Luke 16:31)."* If we won't bother to read God's remedy, then even a resurrection miracle can't shake us.

Oblivious, the proverbial frog in the pot of warming water, we're content to not consider His Word as our cure, comfortably numb as we slow-boil to death. I've reasoned for two years with a cousin who is not a Christian, answering his questions in great detail, but finally this week he told me he is not persuaded. Loved my answers, they all made perfect sense, and was impressed by my knowledge of the Scriptures, but he's decided to take his chances that this world is all there is. Proved, but not convinced.

45

Heartbreaking, but God loves us enough to let us choose — seek Him or ignore Him (Acts 17:30). He will not force a robotic love. We must want His gift of eternal life. My cousin has chosen to ignore the unseen world, and so now I ask you. Will you consider the real world or just sit in the boiling water, happy with what you can only see? In short, do you think Jesus lied to you? (He discusses Truth in the Gospel of John, chapter 8.)

I left my cousin with two questions: *"Is the Bible a supernatural revelation?"* and *"Is Jesus' tomb in Jerusalem empty?"* Disprove those points and then *"eat, drink, and be merry for tomorrow we die."* But if you seek Him out, He promises you'll meet Him (Jeremiah 29:12-13). Perhaps try reading the Book of Romans in a modern translation (*NLT* or *NIV*). The Apostle Paul lays out the Jesus cure very succinctly to the Roman believers.

Reading Romans will only take an hour. I bet it will surprise you, and hopefully change your ending. Remember, deceived means you don't know you're deluded. Surprise endings can be great fun, unless you're the one tricked...like Dr Crowe.

Week 23:
Leo Katzenberger:
"Nicht Schuldig"

"For You, Lord, are good, and ready to forgive, and abundant in mercy to all who call upon You (Psalm 86:5)."

After World War II, not one of the top Nazi defendants pled "Guilty" at the Nuremberg Trials. How blind can you be when the whole world charges you with mass murder? *Judgment at Nuremberg,* written by Abby Mann, won him an Oscar for this 1961 film that dealt with their culpability – were they guilty or just following orders (deceived)?

Burt Lancaster is brilliant as Ernst Janning, a corrupt German judge who sentenced a Jewish man (76) to death for alleged sex with a German woman (30) under their "race-mixing" laws. Ernst bravely rejects his own counsel's argument on his behalf, and admits he was a bad judge who knew the defendant was totally innocent:

"It was the old, old story of the sacrificial lamb. We who know our guilt must admit it. Whatever the pain and humiliation." Ernst Janning's character is based on a true story from March 13, 1942. Both Leo Katzenberger and Irene Seiler denied the charges and said their longstanding friendship was more like a Father helping his daughter. She got two years of hard labor for perjury and his head was chopped off. Janning continues:

"My counsel would have you believe we were not aware of the concentration camps. Not aware? Where were we? Where were we when Hitler began shrieking his hate in the Reichstag? Where were we when our neighbors were being dragged out in the middle of the night to Dachau? Where were we when every village in Germany has a railroad terminal where cattle cars were filled with children being carried out to their extermination! Where were we when they cried out in the night? Deaf, dumb, blind!

"My counsel says we were not aware of the extermination of millions. He would give you the excuse: We were only aware of the extermination

of the hundreds. Does that make us any less guilty? Maybe we didn't know the details. But if we didn't know, it was because we didn't want to know." His honest testimony stands out against the rest.

The Bible says the same…we're all guilty (Romans 3:23). Our first step to be forgiven takes real Janning courage to be as honest. In the eyes of a holy, perfect, and loving God, we are condemned. We will all be judged righteously — not by a crooked judge like Ernst Janning, but by a righteous Judge (2 Corinthians 5:10). Don't be Nazi-blind; deceived, and think *"I'm not that bad."* Compared to Hitler maybe not, but next to God?

Holiness is His standard. *"For whoever keeps the whole Law and yet stumbles in one point, he has become guilty of all* (James 2:10).*"* One sin means not holy, *"guilty of all,"* but one Savior means holy, *"Not Guilty at all* (2 Corinthians 5:21).*"* Throw yourself on the mercy of the court, and you'll find the Lord *"ready to forgive."* Only then can you be declared holy, *"Nicht Schuldig,"* by Jesus Christ, *"the sacrificial Lamb"* (Isaiah 53). Of course, one who thinks they are innocent and pleads *"Not Guilty"* needs no salvation.

Week 24:
Schwinners and Losers

"What does it profit a man to gain the whole world, and lose his soul (Mark 8:36)?"

It was 1970-something. When I stepped out of the *Ben Franklin Variety Store,* my bike was gone! Where I had parked it was now a gaping, empty nothing. My Detroit school bus could have fit sideways in my mouth at that moment. My treasure had vanished!

It was no ordinary bike — a sky blue *Schwinn Stingray,* with a chrome shock-absorber under tall *Fastback* handle bars, a white *Silver-Glow* banana seat on a raised sissy bar over a fat *Slik* rear tire, and the super-cool small, sporty front wheel — it was my baby.

This was my rude awakening to the world of thieves that I lived in. Bad people existed in the shadows that meant me harm. I was sick at heart. I had been violated. I stood there staring at nothing for a long time. It was a turning point for me, and a very long, sad walk home. My prized possession was gone forever, along with my kid-dom innocence.

My own kids joke now that eventually any conversation with me will end up mentioning my adult treasures—the Civil War or Bob Dylan. I happily confess it's true. I love them, but my first love takes precedence, Jesus. Dwight Moody sums all of this up in two lines:

"It does not take long to tell where a man's treasure is. In fifteen minutes' conversation with most men, you can tell whether their treasures are on earth or in Heaven."

People freely talk about their loves, what they treasure, and it's almost immediate. In minutes, we all divulge what's in our heart, but my point concerns protecting that treasure because sooner or later, someone will take it away from you…riches, possessions, family, even your life. The secret to keeping your treasure safe requires valuing the right things.

Jesus tells us in Matthew 6:19-21, *"Do not lay up for yourselves treasures on earth, where moth and rust destroy and where thieves break in and*

steal, but lay up for yourselves treasures in Heaven, where neither moth nor rust destroys and where thieves do not break in and steal. For where your treasure is, there your heart will be also."

Don't be shortsighted and think that this earth is heart-worthy. It's not. Security here is a fallacy. This can all be taken away. Only eternal things are worth your heart's tug. Which begs the question...what then is eternal treasure? I'm no theologian, but God's Word claims to be eternal (Isaiah 40:8) and it says a soul is forever too (Matthew 25:48).

But we have a problem — our hearts are sick (Jeremiah 17:9), infected with a fatal cancer (Romans 6:23, Ephesians 2:1), and only a perfect blood "transfusion" is the antidote (Hebrews 10:14). We think doing good things negates our failures, but it doesn't (Titus 3:5). Only Jesus can regenerate dead heart tissue (Ephesians 1:13-14). You may not love Bob Dylan or the Civil War, but without Jesus (inside your body) whatever you love goes away in the end and leaves a gaping, empty nothing... just like my *Schwinn Stingray.*

Week 25:
Reservations Matter

"I am going the way of all the earth
(King David, 1 Kings 2:1-2)."

"Do you think we can land a helicopter in your yard?" This was a
question I never thought I'd ever hear, especially by a policeman. It was
a shock. Crazy. All of it was.

I had just extinguished the fire in this horrible vehicle wreck at the end
of our driveway. It was dark, chaotic, and scary, but soon enough our
road was filled with fire engines, ambulances, and police cars. It was
clear that there were fatalities. Something else was also clear too.

As I stood there, helpless, watching the Jaws of Life twisting metal, I
thought the only thing that makes sense right now, that matters, is the
gospel message. They were gone. I am going. You are going. Like King
David, we are all going away. Reservations matter.

The Bible makes it clear – crystal, 100 percent clear – that we can know
for sure how to get to Heaven. It is not a guessing game. It is a sure
hope. Consider the Apostle John who saw Jesus die and come back to
life, as much an eyewitness as I was that night:

*"He who has the Son has the life; he who does not have the Son of God
does not have the life. These things I have written to you who believe in
the name of the Son of God, in order that you may know that you have
eternal life* (1 John 5:12-13)."

John says that we can know for sure, and that there are two types of
people – those who have the Son and those who do not. This is not
an intellectual nod to some fact; it involves your will. A white flag
surrender, kneeling in your heart, submitting to the King of kings
in faith, in His death. The result? A Spirit invasion, like a demon
possession, but with a righteous spirit, the Holy Spirit. He will literally
enter your body, as Paul says:

"In Him, you also, after listening to the message of truth, the gospel of your salvation – having also believed, you were sealed in Him with the Holy Spirit of promise, who is given as a pledge of our inheritance, with a view to the redemption of God's own possession, to the praise of His glory (Ephesians 1:13-14)."

His Spirit is a pledge, a down payment, that God will keep His promise to redeem you from death. It's as if God has deposited $599,000 dollars on a $600,000 home. He has pledged to buy it. He's not walking away, in too deep with blood money. His blood.

Jesus said, *"Truly, truly I say to you, he who hears My word, and believes Him who sent Me, has eternal life, and does not come into judgment, but has passed out of death into life* (John 5:24)." Death is dead? My death? Yours? Yes, absolutely (Romans 6:23)!

Sounds nuts? Like asking to land a helicopter in your yard, but this question is not: *"Is the Holy Spirit inside of your body right now?"* If not, don't kid yourself. The Bible says you do not have eternal life. You're definitely going, so why not ask Him to come inside and rescue you. It's a simple 911 call (Romans 10:13). Reservations matter.

Week 26:
The Frozen Custard

"Taste and see that the Lord is good (Psalm 34:8)."

WARNING! This is not a myth. It is a real frozen confection that will change your life.

How can I persuade you that you have not enjoyed the greatest frozen treat on the planet, (unless you have tasted a waffle cone packed and swirled high with frozen custard)? It is not ice cream. It is creamed ice crystals on nuclear steroids, hard to find nowadays, and by far the most luscious treat ever invented! How do I convince you this is true?

I could explain the history of this smooth glory — an invention of Elton and Archie Kohr in 1919 that changed lives at New York's *Coney Island* after they sold over 18,000 cones in just two days. But just explaining their sweet story will not be enough to sway you.

Perhaps divulge the secret recipe of sugar, milk, salt, and egg yolks or dissect the magical machine that concocts this chilled joy spurted into a cone? Probably still not convincing. For this silky smooth miracle to happen, you have to physically try it. You must taste it.

Likewise, the only way to know Jesus is to taste Him, to invite Him into your life, *"that if you confess with your mouth Jesus as Lord and believe in your heart that God raised him from the dead, you will be saved; for with the heart a person believes, resulting in righteousness, and with the mouth he confesses, resulting in salvation* (Romans 10:9-10).*"* That experience involves your heart, and your mouth, which is a cosmic problem.

Imagine if I smeared frozen custard over the face of a coffin-bound corpse, force-feeding this delightful treat onto a tight, rigor mortised mouth. The Bible says that this is our spiritual condition — dead to the things of God, numb to His Frozen Custard salvation.

"And you were dead in your trespasses and sins (Ephesians 2:1).*"* The Bible says we are all corpses, spiritually dead because of our sin, empty

waffle cones. Jesus came to fill those cones with Himself, with a life-giving rich sweetness that results in everlasting delight. So why bother, to come and die a horrible death on a Roman cross?

"But God, being rich in mercy, because of His great love with which He loved us, even when we were dead in our transgressions, made us alive together with Christ. For by grace you have been saved through faith; and that not of yourselves, it is the gift of God; not as a result of works, so that no one may boast (Ephesians 2:5, 8-9)."

God's love is hard to comprehend until you realize there was nothing we could do to fill our empty cone. Only Jesus can fill that void. Only Jesus rose from the dead. Salvation cannot be earned. The empty cone cannot do anything, except choose to be filled. You must open your dead heart and pry your clenched teeth open to receive Him (John 1:12).

There is one real frozen custard shop near us (in Ovid) and there is one real Jesus (in the pages of the New Testament), but you must choose…to open your mouth (Psalm 81:10).

Week 27:
Have You Prayed for
Ozzy Today?

"For the eyes of the Lord are upon the righteous, and His ears attend to their prayer (1 Peter 3:12)."

I've often wondered if anyone is praying for me. Have you thought about that for yourself? On the whole planet, has anyone thought enough about you today to take a few minutes to ask God to help you?

And that brings me to John Michael "Ozzy" Osbourne. My son and I went to see a *Black Sabbath* concert last year (he wanted to see a classic heavy metal band from my era), and while we waited for them to take the stage I wondered if anyone prays for them. So I did.

During that concert I prayed for their salvation. It was kinda' fun to know you can ask God to affect people, despite distance or access, and they can't stop you from intervening for them. So why not save *Black Sabbath?* Ozzy Osbourne, Tony Iommi, Bill Ward, and Geezer Butler need Jesus too, the real "Iron Man." It was humbling to know God heard.

As believers, we have access to His throne at any time to ask for any thing. Amazing!

"Therefore, since we have a great high priest who has passed through the heavens, Jesus the Son of God, let us hold fast our confession. For we do not have a high priest who cannot sympathize with our weaknesses, but One who has been tempted in all things as we are, yet without sin. Therefore let us draw near with confidence to the throne of grace, so that we may receive mercy and find grace to help in time of need (Hebrews 4:14-16)."

This imagery reminds me of JFK and all of the pictures of his kids playing at his feet in the *Oval Office* under his desk. I bet they didn't hesitate to ask their Presidential Dad for anything...because they knew he'd *"help in time of need."* They knew Dad loved them.

I'd like to challenge you to pray for the lost, even famous people you admire are within His influence. Ask God to make them curious and to meet genuine Christians to help answer their questions. God is not limited (1 Samuel 14:6). Nor are you.

Black Sabbath's final tour this past summer means they are approaching the end, and as far as I can tell (from a distance), no one in *Black Sabbath* has met Jesus Christ. They will be dead soon and despite their "God and Satan" gimmick as a band, they need prayer...like all of us. Our heavenly Father loves them, as Ozzy's Dad demonstrated.

As the band's success grew, occultists wanted them to come to their black rituals, but when they declined curses were levied on the band. Ozzy's Father stepped in. Thomas Osbourne worked at a metal factory and made huge crosses for each band member to wear as "protective jewelry." When his Dad died in 1977, Ozzy knew Dad loved him.

So I'm going to pray for them, and a lot of other people I don't have a relationship with, like Presidents, famous athletes, or actors like Brad Pitt and Kevin Costner, and I'd encourage you to do the same. And if you don't know if anyone prays for you, maybe start asking people to put you on their prayer list. It's humbling to do, but why not ask?

It'd be a shame to waste access to the most powerful Person in the history of the world, who wants to help you, and you don't rush into His throne room, hop up on His lap like His only child, and ask for help (Matthew 7:7-11). After all, Dad loves them.

Week 28:
Why Bother...Him?

"Now He was telling them a parable to show that at all times they ought to pray and not to lose heart, saying, 'In a certain city there was a judge who did not fear God and did not respect man. There was a widow in that city, and she kept coming to him, saying, 'Give me legal protection from my opponent.' For a while he was unwilling; but afterward he said to himself, 'Even though I do not fear God nor respect man, yet because this widow bothers me, I will give her legal protection, otherwise by continually coming she will wear me out.'" And the Lord said, "Hear what the unrighteous judge said; now, will not God bring about justice for His elect who cry to Him day and night, and will He delay long over them? I tell you that He will bring about justice for them quickly. However, when the Son of Man comes, will He find faith on the earth (Luke 18:1-8)?"

I've learned three "very" things about prayer. Prayer can be very confusing, very difficult, and very humbling (after all, we're admitting we need His help). Jesus cleared it up with a story about our corruption, God's goodness, and how problems restore us.

Prayer can be confusing because we know the answer is not always yes, but we also know God loves us and wants to help. Wouldn't a yes be helpful? No, just because we ask doesn't make it the right thing or the right timing. Every parent knows this. A "wrong" answer requires trust that our Father knows best, which I learned through a pal.

As a teen, my buddies had mini-bikes, sturdy motorized scooters that went about 40 mph, illegally zipping down our Detroit streets. I nagged my folks for one, but like the *Red Ryder BB Gun* refrain from the movie *A Christmas Story*, *"You'll break your leg"* is all they said (and then my pal Jeff did just that when a car hit him and ruined his summer!).

God is not a cosmic vending machine. He's a loving, sovereign Father. Bugging Him shows our sincerity and genuine desire (unlike that infatuated kid in the checkout line who wants candy, then gum, or on a whim a mini-bike). Wants come and go, but a need is different. Enter Jesus' pugilistic parable on persistence sifting a want from a need.

In one corner is a crooked heavyweight judge, taking bribes, perhaps bribes against the grieving widow, who is also the challenger—a fresh widow, homeless who needs "legal protection" with no husband on the deed with scared, crying children. She's desperate with no choice but to fight. So she goes the distance, 15 brutal rounds until he tosses in the towel (in Greek *"wear me out"* means *"to give a black eye"*).

Prayer sounds like painful, hard, Rocky meet Jack Dempsey work. So why bother? The answer is hidden in the context — the Second Coming (v.8). The Church is like this widow, without her Bridegroom, and seeking help in a world that *"does not fear God nor respect man."* Since Eden, we don't want to seek God, but our needs drive us to Him.

Like any loving Father, He wants us to come back, and that's the answer to why bother him — our needs bring us back home (Luke 15:11-32). That's *A* (real) *Christmas Story*. Coming home to a loving Father, and it all starts with a single prayer. So by all means, bother Him so He finds your *"faith on the earth."* When you're flat on your back, as awful as that can be at times, the only place to look is straight up into Heaven.

Week 29:
Why Be Thankful?

"Oh give thanks to the Lord, for he is good;
for his steadfast love endures forever!"
-King David (1 Chronicles 16)

On October 3, 1863, Abraham Lincoln did something radical that no American President would dare to do today...he declared a national holiday to thank God for His love and blessings on America, despite a raging Civil War with thousands of dead Americans.

Lincoln knew that we were forgetful and focus on the bad things in our lives. He wanted us to remember God's true character – that He is good, loving, and sovereign. Lincoln knew we needed that reminder in a world broken by sin where people have the free will to choose to do horrible things (two months earlier, Gettysburg had over 50,000 casualties).

Despite our wickedness, God remains good and loving toward us. He proved that by sacrificing Jesus to save us (Hebrews 10:14). When we thank God for His many blessings, it changes our mindset to be positive despite our woes (Philippians 4:8). We are quick to forget that He is in charge and He will judge every wrong ever done.

After mentioning all the good things Americans could be thankful for as a nation, Lincoln went on to say this:

"The year that is drawing towards its close has been filled with the blessings of fruitful fields and healthful skies. To these bounties, which are so constantly enjoyed that we are prone to forget the source from which they come, others have been added, which are of so extraordinary a nature, that they cannot fail to penetrate and soften even the heart which is habitually insensible to the ever watchful providence of Almighty God.

"They are the gracious gifts of the Most High God, who, while dealing with us in anger for our sins, hath nevertheless remembered mercy. It has seemed to me fit and proper that they should be solemnly, reverently

*and gratefully acknowledged as with one heart and one voice by the
whole American People.*

*"I do therefore invite my fellow citizens in every part of the United
States, and also those who are at sea and those who are sojourning in
foreign lands, to set apart and observe the last Thursday of November
next, as a day of Thanksgiving and Praise to our beneficent Father who
dwelleth in the Heavens.*

*"And I recommend to them that while offering up the ascriptions justly
due to Him for such singular deliverances and blessings, they do also,
with humble penitence for our national perverseness and disobedience,
commend to His tender care all those who have become widows,
orphans, mourners or sufferers in the lamentable civil strife in which
we are unavoidably engaged, and fervently implore the interposition
of the Almighty Hand to heal the wounds of the nation and to restore
it as soon as may be consistent with the Divine purposes to the full
enjoyment of peace, harmony, tranquility and Union."*

So why be thankful when there's 50,000 reasons to complain this
Thanksgiving? Watch the 2013 film *The Ultimate Life* with James
Garner and Peter Fonda, and let your heart soften up a bit. Pay special
attention to the railroad car scene on September 3, 1941 when a train
jumper changes the main character's life with his "10 Things" that he's
grateful to God for every day.

With Mark Twain wisdom he sets the future billionaire straight with
one golden line you should never forget, no matter how many casualties
come your way, *"You gotta' be grateful for the little things in life,
otherwise you'll never be grateful for nothin'."*

Week 30:
An Understandable
Misunderstanding

"God makes a home for the lonely; He leads out the prisoners into prosperity, only the rebellious dwell in a parched land (Psalm 68:6)."

John Steinbeck, who won a Pulitzer Prize for his novel about a parched land *(The Grapes of Wrath)* said, *"We are lonesome animals. We spend all of our life trying to be less lonesome."*

Put another way, we fill up our Saturdays with some "thing" to not be so lonely. We may not admit it, but we all live for our particular thing... golf, college football, travel, a boat, or a person. And those 3,600 Saturdays all add up to one thing — one life spent, on self.

But the Apostle Paul said, *"To live is Christ."* His "thing" was others, to tell everyone that our death riddle was solved in the resurrected Jesus. *"I do all things for the sake of the gospel."* His life was spent sharing a message to end loneliness and free prisoners.

We think this life is all there is and so we invest in it to stave off our loneliness. Paul disagreed. The real life is yet to come, so death is actually a gain. His full quotation is, *"To live is Christ, and to die is gain."* No one thinks death is a gain. When we offer our condolences we say, *"I'm sorry for your loss."* But Paul says just the opposite, and more!

"I prefer to be absent from the body and at home with the Lord." Death (absent from the body) is preferable when you realize that Jesus Christ is truly alive, and waits for you to come home to the real world (no loneliness), to real "prosperity" (death-row prisoners ransomed and adopted by a cosmic billionaire). If you let Him, He'll lead you home too.

We're lonely because we don't know our Creator, filling up Saturdays in our prison cell with our "thing." We misunderstand. This life is a "puff of smoke." The next eternal life, where the risen Jesus is, is the real deal.

It's an "understandable misunderstanding" because sin has deadened us, made us spiritually unaware of His love, and condemned us.

This sin-coma imprisons us in its death sentence. *"The wages of sin is death,"* both now, making us spiritually dead and separated from God; and also in our physical death, forever separated. But if we give up, ask Him to take away our sin-tattoo, and trust His cross-payment for our sin... then we're released from prison (John 5:24). It's simple faith...a complete, genuine surrender that says, *"I was wrong, I'm sorry, take me back."*

Sadly, Steinbeck rejected Jesus' offer. *"I am not religious so I have no apprehension of the hereafter, either in hope of reward or a fear of punishment."* In 1968, Steinbeck died in New York City, on the Friday before Christmas...hours before his very last Saturday.

Now you know the truth. There's no misunderstanding. You can end your aloneness, come home, and be freed from the sin prison of selfishness. Or stay a rebel like Steinbeck in a parched land, condemned in your cell, waiting for your last Saturday.

Week 31:
That Bloody Vending Machine

"Do not marvel at this; for an hour is coming in which all who are in the tombs shall hear His voice, and shall come forth...(John 5:28-29)."

Since 1978, there have been almost 40 deaths from vending machines. Death is complicated enough, but to die by tilting a vending machine on top of you really takes the *Tasty-kake*. We are told death is natural, right? Wrong. Death is not natural. Death is the most un-natural thing I can think of — we stupidly pulled it down on top of ourselves.

The Bible says death is the result of sin, our rebellion against God. *"The wages of sin is death* (Romans 6:23).*"* We earned death by our rejection of God's best for us. Even today we mostly ignore God as irrelevant. *"The soul who sins will die* (Ezekiel 18:4, 20).*"* Sin changed the natural course of His loving will for us and death was conceived.

But death also focuses us. Our life can seem busy or dull, but seeing death up close changes us. We think deeper and wonder, *"Where is that soul I knew so well?"* We see their body, but we know it's only a clay shell. King Solomon said, *"It is better to go to funerals than parties because death is the end of every man and the living take it to heart."*

Death silences us too. No one has an answer for this bizarre event. When we stare at a loved one in a coffin, and smell decay...no one can comfort our blurry grief. No one, that is, except Jesus, the Son of David. *"I am the resurrection and the life. He who believes in Me shall live even if he dies* (John 11:25).*"* Easter defanged death's bite.

So His death saves us. That's why His words are a marvel to those in the tombs. All the dead will hear Him...and come forth to give an account for their life. The resurrection of the dead is as sure as death stalking you today, and so is His voice to call you to judgment. Jesus earned the right when He rose again and killed death (Revelation 1:18).

Bob Dylan wrote, *"Do you ever wonder just what God requires? You think He's just an errand boy to satisfy your wandering desires."* We

treat God like a vending machine. We think if we pull a cosmic lever then He'll do our bidding. But what does God want? *"For I take no pleasure in the death of anyone who dies,"* declares the Lord God. *"Therefore, repent and live* (Ezekiel 18:32).*"* He wants to restore us, but our sin remains.

Sin made a chasm between God and us (Isaiah 59:2). We need to repent (admit we've blown it), put our sin on Jesus, and take His blood sacrifice to bridge this gap (2 Corinthians 5:21). But how? Vending means *"to transfer to another person the equivalent."* We must make a transfer, and receive Him by faith (Colossians 1:13-14).

You can look at a *Tasty-kake* all day, but it's not yours until you pull the lever...His blood for your sin. Then His voice will be a joyous thrill to hear on that last day, if today is your salvation day (2 Corinthians 6:2).

Week 32:
The Nudge

"Be still, and know that I am God (Psalm 46:10)."

"You never know what may cause them. The sight of the Atlantic Ocean can do it, or a piece of music, or a face you've never seen before. A pair of somebody's old shoes can do it.... You can never be sure. But of this you can be sure. Whenever you find tears in your eyes, especially unexpected tears, it is well to pay the closest attention. They are not only telling you something about the secret of who you are, but more often than not God is speaking to you through them of the mystery of where you have come from and is summoning you to where, if your soul is to be saved, you should go next."

Frederick Buechner wrote that in *"Beyond Words."* It's a warning to the foolishness of being too busy and missing God's quiet nudge. Busyness drowns out the nudge.

The supreme time that is jam-packed with busyness is right now, a dangerous stretch between Thanksgiving and Christmas, which is a shame because we miss the point of both holidays in our attempt to celebrate them. And the sad thing about that hamster wheel is that Jesus is the point of these holidays, and like Martha we miss Him altogether in our busyness (Luke 10:38-42). Why are they so significant?

Thanksgiving is a reflection on our past year. It's meant to contract our busy and divided heart into the united position of thankfulness for His kindnesses. Like the Pilgrim Edward Winslow's observation, despite all of our past difficulties, *"By the goodness of God, we are far from want."* Thankfulness gets you through all the messes of life because you're acknowledging His sovereignty. You are grateful for His guiding hand.

Christmas is different. It's a reminder that life is not about death, but about being rescued from it. God Himself became flesh to die for our sins and restore us to Himself. The Incarnation; God with us. Like the carol says, *"To save us all from Satan's power when we had gone astray."* One holiday looks back and the other looks forward.

Or as Buechner wrote about looking forward, *"Where...you should go next."* An interesting phrase that is as innocent as a blossom, but as profound as the rings of Saturn. *"Where you should go next,"* means after you die and your "next" is a titanic choice.

Accepting a Christmas gift is a choice too, but it's not yours until you receive it. His Christmas gift is a new start, as John 1:12 says, *"But as many as received Him, to them He gave the right to become children of God, even to those who believe in His name."*

So maybe quiet your holiday busyness and just take a walk with Him. Perhaps a stroll in a snowy wood or some lonely path around a lake, and ponder this question about your "next" and where it is...

"If I died tonight, am I one hundred percent certain I'd go to Heaven?" If you're not positive, why not receive His Christmas gift and make Thanksgiving an every day thing?

Week 33:
The Law (and Promise) of Return

"When all these blessings and curses I have set before you come on you and you take them to heart wherever the Lord your God disperses you among the nations, and when you and your children return to the Lord your God and obey him with all your heart and with all your soul according to everything I command you today, then the Lord your God will restore your fortunes and have compassion on you and gather you again from all the nations where he scattered you (Deuteronomy 30:1-3)."

On May 14, 2018, Israel celebrated its 70th anniversary. In 1948, after 2,000 years of wandering, and many more under the rule of other nations, the Jews were back in their biblical homeland as the independent state of Israel. This was a major turning point in history that cannot be underestimated, and it was also prophetic (Jeremiah 16:14-15).

Despite this statehood miracle, there were less than 725,000 Jews in Israel in 1948. Today, however, there are almost 8 million Jews in Israel, and in 2014, another landmark occurred—the number of Jews in Israel passed the number of Jews living in the rest of the world! What fostered this dramatic population explosion that continues unabated today (Isaiah 11:11-12)?

On July 5, 1950, the governing body of Israel, the *Knesset*, passed the "Law of Return," which began with the remarkable words that would define the country's core value: *"Every Jew has the right to immigrate to this country...."*

This law not only populated Israel, but it provided a safe haven from the anti-Semitism that peaked in Hitler's Europe. Despite overt opposition and wars, it's been a remarkable catalyst to grow Israel and make her desert bloom around thriving, modern cities. But can the "Law of Return" be solely responsible for this miracle? Not hardly. It was God, and His repeated promises in the Old Testament.

67

Watching these immigrants arrive at *Ben Gurion Airport* is like seeing a biblical prophecy unfold when you consider the prophecies of Jeremiah (16:15, 23:3,7-8, 30:1-11, 31:9, 33:7), Isaiah (43:5-6, 49:8-22, 54:7), and especially Ezekiel (11:17, 20:34, 28:25, 34:13, 37:21). I've seen it firsthand and it's a big celebration each time!

In chapter 37, Ezekiel had a vision of a valley filled with the dry bones of thousands of skeletons in open graves. These bones came together, grew flesh, and came to life. God revealed that the dry bones symbolized Israel and her agonies of dispersion for rejecting Him. The graves were Gentile nations where they were banished, but they were only temporary, open graves. The coming together of the resurrected bones is the prophetic restoration of the dispersed nation to its biblical homeland.

At the 65th anniversary of the liberation of *Auschwitz*, Benjamin Netanyahu ended his speech by quoting Ezekiel 37:11-13 as being fulfilled! This physical restoration of Israel is amazing, but the next verse promises more…a spiritual restoration. The "Law of Return" is part of a major turning point in history, but verse 14 will be the consummation of God's promise for Israel when they finally recognize their Messiah (Ezekiel 36:26-28).

Week 34:
The Exorcist...Reversed

"Test yourselves to see if you are in... (2 Corinthians 13:5)."

Deliver the message. That was my job at *Knight-Ridder Newspapers* for four years.

As the Home Delivery Manager, I made sure you got your newspaper on time and readable (dry), 365 days a year. Sounds easy, right? Just trust my six District Managers, to trust 42 drivers and 350 kids to follow directions, in the dark, with 30,000 newspapers.

Frankly, it was hard, and a lot like life...a daily test, challenges galore, and trusting others to deliver. If that sounds familiar, and your life's hard, then consider reading the directions — the Bible. I know, it sounds corny, but God's Instruction Manual has one primary wow-message: Life makes the most sense if the Author is inside of your body.

You read that right, God...in...you. The Apostle Paul said, *"Test yourselves to see if you are in the faith; examine yourselves! Or do you not recognize this about yourselves that Jesus Christ is in you — unless indeed you fail the test."* That's what it means to be a Christian, Christ in you, literally. Jesus wants to possess your body with His Spirit.

I never knew that being a Christian meant Jesus inside of me until I read Ephesians 1:13-14. Hear His message, believe it, and then be permanently sealed — God's Spirit living in my body. The coolest thing (and there are lots of cool things) is that this Spirit possession makes you immortal! Sounds crazy, right? Well, that's what Jesus said (John 14:16-20). He's either lying, totally insane, or exactly who He said... God-in-the-flesh.

God's message is simple: *"Jesus can be embedded in you."* You don't have to be alone in life. But believing in God (in His existence or facts about Him) doesn't make you a Christian. There's only one question on His test about who goes to Heaven...have you asked Jesus to come inside of you? *"Christ in you, the hope of glory* (Colossians 1:27).*"*

It has nothing to do with you or your religion. Nothing. Being good or bad, an American or going to church, baptized, Catholic, Protestant, Jewish, Muslim, Hindu, or an atheist. It's just this...is the resurrected Jesus of Nazareth inside of your physical body now? That's all. Spirit possession. His entrance restores your broken relationship with the Father, obliterates your sin, and gives you a fresh start, a new spiritual birth (John 3:1-3).

That's amazing! The Creator in you, helping you with life's daily challenges, giving you a clear conscience because all of your sins are forgiven, and now your best friend (who has all power, even enough to de-fang death and raise the dead). It's a totally free gift for anyone who asks Him to come inside (Romans 6:23). Just trust Him to deliver you.

And all God wants in return is you. Change your mind about living alone, give up trying, and come home to Dad (Luke 15:11-32). Don't take my word for it. Go read the New Testament in a modern version (like the *New Living Translation*). Well, that's it. My job is done. Message delivered, on time, and readable. Now it's up to you...is He in or out?

Week 35:
POV

"Man looks at the outward appearance, but the Lord looks at the... (1 Samuel 16:7)."

We're all just 12-year-olds in grown-up clothes. That perspective got me through a recent conference full of very important Hollywood folks. We're all just people.

Anyone who knows me knows that I like to talk to strangers. On a vacation once my family didn't know where I was. My daughter said, *"Just look for a crowd and Dad will be in the middle."* I'm used to talking to strangers, but when they wield that much media influence, it puts me off my game a bit. We see the clothes, famous faces, and name tags.

Our human point of view can shift, be influenced, and we all disagree on something, but God is not sidetracked by appearances – He looks inside, at the heart. And so, His POV is right, and always right. We form opinions and views, but God has the heart facts.

And what is God's point of view on us? God's POV on "our facts" is clearly revealed in the Bible. He says we are made in His likeness and each person has great value as His reflection. *"God created Man in His own image, male and female...(Genesis 1:27)."*

But He says we're rebels, lawbreakers, running from Him and His immense love. *"All of us like sheep have gone astray. Each of us has turned to his own way...(Isaiah 53:6)."*

That's because we're all broken by this rebellious, independent, and selfish attitude, what the Bible calls sin. *"All have sinned and fall short of the glory of God (Romans 3:23)."* (Doubt it? Who do you look for first in your school yearbook or family group photos?)

And yet, He loves us anyway, which is quite astounding. *"But God demonstrates His own love toward us in that while we were yet sinners, Christ died for us...(Romans 5:8)."*

He came to rescue us from spiritual death, caused by sin that makes us unholy. *"The Son of Man has come to seek and to save that which was lost* (Luke 19:10, Romans 6:23)."

He also says that if we don't return, that one day He'll punish everyone who defies Him and His Word. *"Be sure of this: The wicked will not go unpunished* (Proverbs 11:21)."

Our punishment is just, and loving (because it protects those who love Him from harm). *"Dealing out retribution to those who do not know God and to those who do not obey the gospel of our Lord Jesus. These will pay the penalty of eternal destruction, away from the presence of the Lord and from the glory of His power* (2 Thessalonians 1:8-9)."

He does not delight in our death or our rebellion. *"I take no pleasure in the death of the wicked, but rather that the wicked turn from his way and live...(Ezekiel 33:11)."* It's all very bad news, and thankfully really good news. I guess it all depends on our point of view on how we see God's POV. After all, most 12-year-olds in adult clothes know best.

Week 36:
Our Dad Who Art in Heaven

"For this reason I say to you, do not be worried about your life, as to what you will eat or what you will drink; nor for your body, as to what you will put on. Is not life more than food, and the body more than clothing? Look at the birds of the air, that they do not sow, nor reap nor gather into barns, and yet your heavenly Father feeds them. Are you not worth much more than they (Matthew 6:25-26)?"

Some say we view our heavenly Father through the lens of our earthly Father. A sort of imprinting from their characteristics in how they raised us, whether generous or severe, a dictator or absent, distant or close; all of it affects how you see God now. Since we just honored Dads with *Father's Day* it seems appropriate to comment on our heavenly Dad.

Jesus described Dad as benevolent, valuing us more than all of His other creation (that incidentally, is never worried; some say we are the only creature who actually does worry about life). When the Disciples were in danger of drowning, Jesus rebuked them for not trusting Dad, and quieted the tempest with a word (Mark 4). So, value dilutes worry.

Dad considers you precious and He will take care of you, even if your life isn't as you think it should be because of real concerns with money, health, or maybe even your own earthly Father's failures. Does Dad in Heaven really see us like this? Jesus goes on,

"And who of you by being worried can add a single hour to his life? And why are you worried about clothing? Observe how the lilies of the field grow; they do not toil nor do they spin, yet I say to you that not even Solomon in all his glory clothed himself like one of these. But if God so clothes the grass of the field, which is alive today and tomorrow is thrown into the furnace, will He not much more clothe you? You of little faith!"

What does this tell us about our Dad in Heaven? That He loves us (or Jesus is a liar)!

"Do not worry then, saying, 'What will we eat?' or 'What will we drink?' or 'What will we wear for clothing?' For the Gentiles eagerly seek all these things; for your heavenly Father knows that you need all these things. But seek first His kingdom and His righteousness, and all these things will be added to you. So do not worry about tomorrow; for tomorrow will care for itself. Each day has enough trouble of its own."

The key to His *"all these things"* promise is to put Dad first, seek and join His Kingdom, and come back under His righteous rule as Lord. Even if you are in the deepest, dirtiest pit, it doesn't mean that Dad stopped loving you. Look at the cross, and you can see He loved you as is, despite what you've done, *"while we were enemies* (Romans 5:8-10)."*

Dad didn't just say it, *"But God demonstrates His own love for us in that while we were yet sinners, Christ died for us."* At your very worst, He still wanted you, and died for you. You're worth so much, more than anything else. There are no worries in His tender care, under His rule as a benevolent dictator, who gave up His own Son just to have you back.

Week 37:
Meeting Alice Cooper

"Let him who boasts boast in this, that he understands and knows Me (Jeremiah 9:24)."

It was 1976…Las Vegas. I was a teenager when I saw Alice Cooper for the first time at the *Aladdin Casino*. The rock legend thundered on stage and Sin-City went berserk!

At the edge of the stage a fan snapped pictures as he sang. Alice leaned over for close ups and she frantically clicked away. Then he grabbed her camera and started taking close ups of her! Alice gave the camera back and went on to give a great performance.

Fabulous memories for her and me. I was not a famous rock star, but Alice and I had one thing in common -- we were both prodigal sons from Detroit, stoners running away from our Father in Heaven. Neither one of us knew or understood God one bit. We were lost.

That changed for me in 1980, and for Alice a bit later when we surrendered to Jesus Christ. *"I was drinking with Jim Morrison, Jimi Hendrix, and trying to keep up with Keith Moon and they all died at 27,"* Cooper said. *"I was throwing up blood nearly every morning."* I was partying too, but with my less famous pals…Cooper, Jimmy, and Keith.

I nearly died too, but the real story is that we both came home to our Father. Jesus saved us, the famous and the not so famous. Last Friday, we finally met. He signed my book—*52 THINKS ABOUT GOD*—and we chatted for a bit. I gave him a copy for his teen center in Phoenix *(Solid Rock)*, which helps kids stay off the streets with free lessons to play instruments, sports, etc. He lit up when I told him the gospel content in my book.

When we finished talking, Alice asked me what I wanted him to sign on the title page of *52 THINKS*. I suggested one of my life verses, *"How about Romans 9:16-17?"*

He grinned a big friendly smile and said, *"How about Galatians 2:20?"*

I winked back. *"Works for me."* He didn't know it, but that's also a life verse for me.

I shared Galatians 2:20 in 1980 at my baptism in the middle of the *Red Cedar River* at *MSU.* Our mutual life verse sums up how you become a Christian (which baptism symbolizes in the death of your old life... buried in the water and then raised up anew).

"I have been crucified with Christ; and it is no longer I who live, but Christ lives in me; and the life that I now live in the flesh I live by faith in the Son of God, who loved me and delivered Himself up for me." Did you catch that? Christ...lives...in...me!

Meeting Alice was a big thrill, but understanding and knowing God is the real boast. Alice and I have that in common. Jesus lives in our bodies. You can meet Alice too, in Heaven. Just surrender and ask Jesus to come inside...and join us, the former prodigals.

Week 38:
Lincoln's Favorite Question

"This mortal must put on immortality...
(1 Corinthians 15:53)."

With about six months to live, Abraham Lincoln revealed his fixation with the poem *"Mortality"* to the American painter, Francis Carpenter. In 1864, he spent six months at the White House painting *The Great Emancipator*. Lincoln never met William Knox, but he liked his words so much that he memorized this poem at a young age. Here is part of it:

O, why should the spirit of mortal be proud!
Like a swift-fleeting meteor, a fast-flying cloud,
A flash of the lightning, a break of the wave,
Man passes from life to his rest in the grave.

The hand of the king that the scepter hath borne;
The brow of the priest that the mitre hath worn;
The eye of the sage and the heart of the brave,
Are hidden and lost in the depth of the grave.

The saint that enjoyed the communion of Heaven,
The sinner that dared to remain unforgiven,
The wise and the foolish, the guilty and just,
Have quietly mingled their bones in the dust.

For we are the same things that our fathers have been,
We see the same sights that our fathers have seen,
We drink the same stream and we feel the same sun,
And we run the same course our fathers have run.

They loved, but the story we cannot unfold;
They scorned, but the heart of the haughty is cold;
They grieved, but no wail from their slumbers will come;
They joyed, but the tongue of their gladness is dumb.

Tis' the wink of an eye, tis' the draught of a breath,
From the blossom of health to the paleness of death,
From the gilded saloon to the bier and the shroud,
O, why should the spirit of mortal be proud!

The Greatest Emancipator – Jesus – died to make us free and immortal. So, why dare *"to remain unforgiven"* when mortals can become immortal? Good question. The answer is in Knox's rhetorical question...pride. We think we're good enough, but compared to a holy God we all fall short (Romans 3:23). We are not good enough. We are broken; thus mortal.

The only solution was God had to die for us, and if we will humble ourselves and receive Him (John 1:12-13), we can be immortal, born twice. Knowing we are mortal, and will die, I ask Lincoln's favorite rhetorical question a third time... *"O, why should the spirit of mortal be proud!"*

Week 39:
Last Words Matter Most

"Now these are the last words of David...(2 Samuel 23:1)."

Try yelling for help in New York City and most likely you'll be drowned out by the noise. Throw a handful of silver dollars on that same busy street in Manhattan and everyone will stop and listen. People hear what they want to hear.

The Bible calls it *"tickling ears"* in regard to hearing truth (2 Timothy 4:3). We all have a bias. Remaining neutral is a real challenge when a message is conveyed. Most of us think we know better. But what if God spoke to you? Could you hear Him? King David said that this actually happened to him. He heard God speak to him, and wrote it down.

"The Spirit of the Lord spoke by me, and His word was on my tongue (2 Samuel 23:2)." King David prefaced this by saying that these were to be his last words, a dying man wanting to convey his very last message. That would tend to be vitally important stuff, right? So important that he says God recorded it here, on these very pages, for you!

The Bible makes this claim — to be a supernatural book, that the first Writer gave to His creation to explain truth. The Apostle Paul wrote, *"All Scripture is inspired by God (2 Timothy 3:16-17)."* If you've ever been too close to someone with bad breath, that made you step back, that is what "inspired" means in the original Greek language. It is so authentic, and so close, that it is like "God-breathed" and you know what gum He chews.

The Bible says of itself that God ordered it to be written down by, as Peter said, *"men moved by the Holy Spirit spoke from God (2 Peter 1:21)."* So what? People "claim" a lot of things, some are nuts, selling something, or worse. How can we know it's God's Word, that we can trust these words to be true, that these 40 writers weren't nuts, and that the Bible printing companies aren't just selling something, or worse?

There are lots of textual criticisms by scholars, archaeological proofs, and prophetic history to corroborate this as a truly divine book. I've

read and studied it for almost 50 years. Lots and lots of evidence that would blow you away...but I don't think any of that matters to most people. We're too busy, too skeptical, and too *"So what?"* But...

What if it is God speaking — the Living God that Moses talked to, and Jesus claimed to be? And what if the whole point was that He wants you to be His friend, to be immortal, and to give you your heart's desire? My best answer to *"So what?"* is read it for yourself. If I'm wrong, then the worst that happens is you read the best selling book of all-time.

If we keep on reading David's words, in verse 5, he explains God's offer is exactly that: *"an everlasting covenant (eternal friendship), salvation (immortality via David's son, Jesus), and your desires fulfilled."* Now ask yourself would his last words really be a lie? I'm just tossing this out there for you to consider...like a handful of noisy, silver dollars.

Week 40:
Isaiah Hark Dude

"I am coming and I will live among you...
(Zephaniah 2:10-11)."

Christmas Eve always held a wonderful magic for me as a small boy. It almost tingled.

There was a midnight church service with carols, incense, and candles, and then home to try to sleep before the cascade of presents filled our living room. I didn't quite understand it all, but Jesus and Santa had a major role. It was like a jigsaw puzzle with no box lid to see how to finish the puzzle, but I got cool toys. That much I understood.

As I got older, that magic faded. I understood more — Santa was my parents and the picture on the lid was a nativity scene of an important baby who would die on a cross, but now I got clothes. For me, Christmas became more like a big birthday. Where was that special magic? I still didn't see how it all fit together. Now the puzzle pieces seemed to be flipped over, all gray. The answer had to be in that other jigsaw puzzle — the Bible.

There was an answer in Isaiah 48:16… *"Draw near to Me, hear this: Since the beginning, I have not spoken in secret. From the time it existed, I was there. So now the Lord God has sent Me, and His Spirit."* So God had intended all along to come to us. Christmas was not a secret (Isaiah wrote this about 700 years before Jesus was born, but God had planned it well before that, from the very beginning of time). Sounds magical, but why?

According to Isaiah, that manger baby in swaddling clothes was sent by God…and was God Himself — Immanuel means *"God with us* (Isaiah 7:14)."* A Christmas carol flashed to mind, *"Veiled in flesh, the Godhead see; hail th'incarnate Deity (Hark! The Herald Angels Sing)."* More lyrics helped flip the puzzle pieces over to see God's big picture, *"God and sinners reconciled!"* Ah, it's about reconciliation with God (Isaiah 61:1-2).

So, the picture on the lid was the Bethlehem nativity, but in the background was the point, Jesus on the cross. Our sin separated us from God (Isaiah 59:2). God came as a baby, the King of all kings, to die for us to end sin and death (Isaiah 53:1-12), *"Born that man no more may die; born to raise the sons of earth, born to give them second birth."* His death would remove our sin, raise us up from the dead like Jesus, and reconnect us to God in a new way (John 3:1-15). So Easter was in Christmas? That's tingle-magic too!

But if Christmas holds no magic for you, and it's all gray, try flipping over these Isaiah pages. You just need to hark…which means, *"Dude! Listen up!"* Or as the Spirit said through Isaiah, *"Come near to Me, listen to this…I have not spoken in secret."* That means Hark, and that's looking up these Bible passages. You can start with Isaiah 9:2-7.

Harking is really that simple. Just read. Christmas is not a secret. Then, just receive His reconciliation gift by faith, like a small child (John 1:12-14). Isaiah. Hark. Dude!

Week 41:
(No) Help Wanted

"The stone which the builders rejected became the most important (Mark 12:1-25)."

Remember your first job? Usually it's not very important, but mine had a nice perk. I worked with movie stars. I don't recall the job posting, but I guess I fit the bill because I got hired — as a busboy at a private tennis club serving famous people like Bill Cosby.

Now suppose God wanted to hire somebody, what would that job description look like? God doesn't need anything, but what if it was for us, to solve a problem we had? Isaiah 53:6 says, *"All we like sheep have gone astray, each of us has turned to his own way."* We've all lied, cheated, or stolen. So what? Nobody's perfect. We're all off the path.

But part of our straying problem is we don't want help. We think we're fine. Sin is no big deal. God says otherwise. *"The wages of sin is death* (Romans 6:23).*"* Nobody's perfect means we all work at Sin, Inc. and our paycheck is death. It killed our soul (Ephesians 2:1), our body (Romans 5:12), and separated us from Him (Isaiah 59:2). Even one sin ruins us (James 2:10). So can't we just say we're sorry and be forgiven?

Not really. Sin is in our nature, like an arsenic tattoo. Just asking for forgiveness doesn't erase the stain. We assume we're forgiven because God loves us, but we forget that He's also righteous (holy), which means He must punish all wrongs to remain just and fair (Exodus 34:7). A righteous God has only one way to remove our death tattoo. Blood.

The animal sacrifices in the Old Testament gave us a clue about the gravity of sin and forgiveness. It's costly, gross, takes a life, and is only a temporary fix (that's why they were repeated). What we need is a permanent fix to make us perfect (holy) to be with a perfect (holy) God. All this blood pointed to a future death to do just that (Hebrews 10).

Since God is the only one who is perfect, only His blood can remove sin, which brings us back to God's Want Ad — *"Wanted, a perfect man to have the iniquity of all put on him. Must be good with rejection."*

God's job posting went unanswered until Jesus arrived (Luke 4:14-21), the only qualified applicant to interview (John 14:6). In short, God's love and justice met on the cross and solved a problem we couldn't fix.

"He made Him (Jesus) who knew no sin to become sin on our behalf that we might become the righteousness of God in Him (2 Corinthians 5:21).*"* Imagine King Charles has to judge Prince Harry for murder. He can't ignore his crime, so he took his place. Sin is a very big deal because the King had to die to remove your tattoo (Romans 5:8).

So how do sheep apply His blood soap? Give up, turn back to God's path, and wash by faith in His mercy as your substitute (John 1:12, Ephesians 2:8-9). His gift of eternal life was expensive, but the good news is it's free at Jesus, Inc. (Romans 6:23). Then, go start your new position, serving the King, raised from the dead (proof sin and death are dead). Oh, and the benefits…quite literally out of this world…that is, if you want help.

Week 42:
God's Big But

> *"He brought me up out of the pit of destruction...*
> *(Psalm 40:2)."*

It was 1947, in bombed-out Munich. A Nazi guard from her own concentration camp, a man who had been an accomplice in killing her dear sister Betsie, who now stood right in front of her...wanted to shake her hand? What absolute madness! Shake hands?

Corrie Ten Boom, whose epic book and movie, *The Hiding Place*, would make her famous after World War II, had just given a talk at a church on God's forgiveness in Christ Jesus — and here was this vicious monster commending her for those words.

"You mentioned Ravensbrück in your talk," he said. *"I was a guard there. But since that time, I have become a Christian. I know God has forgiven me for the cruel things I did there, but I would like to hear it from your lips as well. Fräulein, will you forgive me?"*

Her memories crashed back: a huge room full of naked women, piles of clothes and shoes, harsh lights, and this horrible man in a uniform with the skull and crossbones on his hat. This German butcher! His leather crop swinging from his belt, used so freely to beat them...but now his hand, empty, innocent, outstretched as a brother in the Lord.

Obviously, this story is messed up on so many levels. Two Christian spinsters from Holland arrested for hiding Jews, and 10 days later their Father dead in prison. All three innocent, but this balding, heavyset old man in a gray overcoat, guilty, deserving death...was free and forgiven. This was justice? Where was God in this?

God was in Jerusalem, in the flesh, a perfect-innocent man who also stretched out His hand, and got a spike hammered into it by a Roman thug; then the other hand, and both feet. Whipped, beaten while blindfolded, spit on, stripped naked to hang along a busy road, mocked and laughed at during Passover, by His creation! More madness, but...

God satisfied this justice Himself. *"But God demonstrates His own love toward us in that while we were yet sinners Christ died for us* (Romans 5:8-10)." After a moment, she grasped her enemy's hand, nailed together as one by God's big but — *"the just for the unjust* (1 Peter 3:18)."* She knew Jesus became sin…for them (2 Corinthians 5:21).

We think this Nazi deserved Hell. Unlike him, we're not that bad; pretty good in fact, never doing anything like him, but God says, *"For whoever keeps the whole Law and yet stumbles in one point, he has become guilty of all* (James 2:10)."* Now Corrie was no Nazi thug, but compared to a perfect and holy God, she was guilty too (Isaiah 59:2).

Think you're not that bad, then why did Jesus have to die? *"If righteousness comes through the Law (being good), then Christ died needlessly* (Galatians 2:21)."* And that's real madness; to think you're self-righteous, and a holy God will just ignore your sin. Sin must be a bigger deal than we know if Jesus had to die to get rid of it, and a Nazi's guilt.

Unless you see your own guilt, you'll never understand Corrie's Nazi handshake. God is offering you His hand right now, to pull you out of the pit. You can refuse it, but you can never say you didn't recognize it… it's the one with a hole in it.

Week 43:
Door Stops

"Unless I shall see...I will not believe (John 20:19-25)."

We are skeptical by nature. *"Give them the benefit of the doubt"* is a rarity. Why is that? We've all gotten burned by being too trusting, been taken advantage of, or lied to. Trust can be dangerous. Better to not open that trust door, but I recently stopped to help a guy who broke down on the highway. Potentially, a big risk, but it was the right thing to do.

I got off at the next exit and came back. He'd run out of gas on the way to the doctor with his wife (she had cancer and was inside with their baby). We drove to the next exit and got some gas. He was very grateful, but I was the one who was blessed. It felt good to trust God. You see, he was black, and before I became a Christian, I hated blacks.

I grew up in Detroit and went to an almost all black high school and had gotten kicked out for fighting. I had friends killed by them, been in lots of fights, and even started a riot at our high school because of our mutual prejudice. That all changed when I trusted Christ in 1980. I realized that the color on the outside was irrelevant. The color that mattered was inside, in my heart, and that was very dark indeed (Romans 3:23).

When I left my new friend, he thanked me. We both knew he was in a bad way and that I was an unlikely candidate to stop. He smiled and we went on our way. I'm glad I wasn't skeptical that day. Would you take a chance like that...with God, take Him at His word?

The Bible says He cannot lie, *"In the hope of eternal life, which God, who cannot lie, promised long ages ago...(Titus 1:2)."* God's Word, the Bible, is true — every word of it. It would've been a big mistake if I didn't help that young family, and it's an even bigger mistake, an eternal one, for you not to trust Him when what He's promised is immortality because there's no risk, none whatsoever...it's a free gift (Romans 6:23).

"I am the way, and the truth, and the life; no one comes to the Father, but through Me (John 14:6)." Jesus said He is the only way, but our nature is more like Satan's, we doubt His words. Look what Satan said in Genesis 3:1, *"Has God really said…?"* Behold, the first skeptic, and according to Jesus, Satan is our father, and the father of lies (John 8:44). You probably even doubt that (but now you know why *"we are skeptical by nature"*).

Even Thomas doubted his fellow Apostles who told him Jesus was alive, that is until He walked through a locked door. Jesus is here right now, at the door of your heart. *"Behold, I stand at the door and knock; if anyone hears My voice and opens the door, I will come in to him* (Revelation 3:20)." He has never lied. Not once.

If you doubt that, go read what He said in John's Gospel, chapter 10. It might seem scary, but trust me. Stop doubting Him. Turn around, come back, and answer the door. It's the right thing to do.

Week 44:
Don't Judge A Book...

"No prophet is welcome in his hometown ... (Luke 4:24)."

Looking for something good to watch tonight? You may dismiss my top five movies (they're all in black and white), but trust me...I guarantee you won't regret spending 9.2 hours of your life on these celluloid gems. At the risk of being pre-judged, here goes...

My Exhibit A — *Casablanca* (1942), *It's A Wonderful Life* (1946), *It Happened One Night* (1934), *Arsenic and Old Lace* (1944), and *12 Angry Men* (1957).

If I were on trial, it wouldn't help my case to tell you that each film made under 5 million dollars, but despite their box office evidence... trust me; they're legit winners. Let's look at the biggest flop at a measly 2 million bucks, the courtroom classic — *12 Angry Men*.

A teenager is accused of murdering his Father and all 11 jurors think it's a slam-dunk guilty verdict, except Henry Fonda. Despite the "evidence," Fonda persuades all 11 men to look closer and converts all of them, one at a time. They were all dead wrong and an innocent boy is saved. Fonda's flop, which he called *"magnificent,"* meant he never got paid. Just like the story, where everyone was wrong, he was proven right about his film.

12 Angry Men is now considered the second best courtroom drama behind *To Kill A Mockingbird*, and was nominated or won 15 major awards! Funny how something old, or not a financial success, or too familiar, can be rejected without proper scrutiny. Don't judge a book by its cover. In that light, I give you Exhibit B — the Bible (also in black and white), and often dismissed despite its ability to predict the future (Isaiah 46:8-11).

Consider Cyrus, King of Persia, who beat Babylon, the superpower of his day, without battle by diverting the Euphrates River, and according to Herodotus, the city's watery defenses *"dropped to the height of a man's thigh."* They marched up the riverbed into the city on the night

of October 12, 539 BC. I even saw *The Cyrus Cylinder* in the *British Museum* that records his conquest, what God told Isaiah over 200 years before he did it!

According to Josephus, Daniel (a captive from Babylon's destruction of Jerusalem in 586 BC) showed Cyrus Isaiah's scroll. It called Cyrus by name, said he'd conquer Babylon, and send the Jews back to rebuild Jerusalem, ending their exile after 70 years (also predicted in Jeremiah 25:9-13). Amazed because Isaiah died 150 years before Cyrus was even born, Cyrus freed the Jews (Isaiah 45:1-8, 47:1-15, 44:24-28, 48:1-22; Ezra 1:1-4)!

So why did God do all this? He wants you to know He's legit, and to seek Him (Jeremiah 29:13). Start by reading Isaiah's chapters above (44-48, and then 53 written 700 years before Jesus). Two other great films sum up your choice, *The Searchers* and *The Quiet Man*. You can stay quiet, do nothing, or you can search and seek because there's Fonda-like evidence if you look closer.

If you trusted me on Exhibit A, spend a few more hours of your life on Exhibit B, and maybe you'll go *From Here to Eternity*.

Week 45:
Awaiting Your Reply

"Indeed, has God said...(Genesis 3:1)?"

Forget religion. Those boring things on Sunday, that went over your head, and made yawns miraculously appear. Forget all that stuff. But what if...God, the *"prepare-to-meet-your-Maker"* in the Westerns, spoke to you? Your jaw would drop, but not with a yawn. Now that, partner, would be pretty dang cool! God talked...to you? Wow!

Unfortunately, most of us don't care about God. Not really. Your checkbook and your schedule will tell you what you care about. Our eyes glaze over. Even now, you're close to bailing on me. King Moonracer from *Rudolph the Red-Nosed Reindeer* is more relevant. The Bible confirms our attitude in Romans chapter three, *"There is none who seeks for God."* But...what if...He made the first move and actually did call you?

When I was a kid and heard some crazy statement (God talking to you), our comeback would be, *"Says you!"* Or the more colorful Hollywood version, *"You're full of beans and so's your old man."* Think Flick in *A Christmas Story* film. But again...what if?

The Bible claims that God spoke through men who recorded His words (2 Timothy 3:16 and 2 Samuel 23:2). Satan knows this is true, but he twists it with a flick of his forked tongue. God said in Genesis 2:16-17, *"You shall surely die if you eat from the Tree of the Knowledge of Good and Evil."* Satan didn't deny it, he just questioned God's words, *"Indeed, has God said...?"* Since we all die now, I think we know how this went.

You can ignore this claim, or spin it like Satan, but either God spoke or God did not speak. One is true. One false. The Bible says He supernaturally recorded a message for us in the Hebrew Scriptures. I hear you, *"Says you! Prove it!"* I will offer only one answer, but first here's the message Satan does not want you to look up. Big drum-roll.

Despite ignoring God (Isaiah 53:6), He loved us, and became flesh to tell us in person (John 1:1-14). Jesus came to rescue us, by dying for our indifference (Romans 5:8). Our attitude was a deal-breaker (Romans 3:23) and His death was the only way to save us (John 14:6), but we have to reply (Romans 10:9-13). God says in Isaiah chapter 66, *"I called, but no one answered. I spoke, but they did not listen."* My answer? Lick it.

In *A Christmas Story*, Flick puts his tongue on the frozen flagpole to prove it wouldn't stick. Put your tongue on His tongue, and read it for yourself (the *New Living Translation* reads easy). Now remember, if you accept my challenge, you already know Satan's trick, to question His revelation...so be ready. Try John's Gospel, the fourth book in the New Testament (just a two-hour read). If false, what do you have to lose?

But if you say, *"No thanks, I don't care,"* then Romans would be a good second read because your tongue is already stuck (*"There is none who seeks for God."*). Remember, not boring religion. God spoke to you, and you only have to listen (Jeremiah 29:12-13).

Week 46:
A Door, A Jar

*"He is in the monstrous deep. There is nothing beneath
his feet but the yielding, fleeing element."*
(Victor Hugo, "Les Miserables")

What made hospitals smell so bad?

I stepped off the elevator and turned left. It wouldn't be long now. The doctors thought Monday at the latest. We hadn't discussed it much, not at all really. Perhaps that was my fault. Maybe it was mutual. Probably wishful thinking on both our parts; trying to ignore the inevitable, I guess. But we both knew it now. You could feel it in the room the last time. It was almost like "it" was an unseen person. We couldn't pretend anymore. Sort of eerie, like something was slipping away, something that you couldn't stop. I was glad that I'd taken the time to write it all down. With a deep, unconscious breath, I pushed against his heavy door.

"How ya' feelin' today?" I asked with a cautious smile, pulling up a chair. It felt awkward and stiff.

"Not much different." He sighed heavily. *"Physically, anyway."* He seemed to know how bad he looked.

He was very matter-of-fact. No real emotion. Almost as if he'd just resigned a chess match. I probed a bit more.

"Are you afraid at all? I mean, have you thought about...."

"Yeah. I guess." He cut me off, thankfully. *"More like curious excitement mixed up with...fear."*

There was a long, long silence. And then, just as I opened my mouth, he spoke again. Slow and deliberate.

"Ya' know, Phil." His voice cracked a little. *"We've never really talked about dying, not in a real way. Whaddya' think's gonna' happen first? I mean, as a pastor, what do you think goes on? Will I see Him...right away?"* Our eyes met. Mine watered. I think I sniffled a little too.

93

That's when I handed it to him, the same paper you're reading now. It felt like it weighed 50 pounds, then.

I cleared my throat. *"I thought it might be easier to read about it, instead of trying to talk about it; so I put this together."* I lifted it up tentatively toward his bed, not sure if he'd want it. His eyes fell on the first sentence.

In the movie *Patton*, with George C. Scott, the General is reflecting on the glory of battle and makes a stunning remark to one of his officers. Amidst the haze of battle smoke, he says, *"Did you ever stop to think that death might be more exciting than life?"* What an amazing statement to make on a battlefield strewn with dead and dying men! The quote is true, but I made up the scene. But this is what the Apostle Paul said in Philippians, *"To depart and be with Christ, for that is very much the better."* And in Second Corinthians, *"To be absent from the body is to be present with the Lord."*

Is it possible that to be dead is a good thing? No, a great and wonderful thing? That's what Patton wondered. Is it just a door to a better existence with more wonder than this shadow we call "life?" So what does happen at the precise moment of death? In that twinkle of a millisecond when our heart has just beat and pumped its last, what actually takes place? I've often wondered about it, passing into the world of spirits and vacating our clay jar. What actually occurs in that first sliver of true timelessness?

Perhaps it's something like this….

Week 47:
A Door, A Jar II

"I called out of my distress to the Lord, and He answered me. I cried for help from the depth of Sheol: Thou didst hear my voice (Jonah 2:2)."

A searing flash of light so bright that your eyes are useless, but you can see it all! You can make out what you know to be your close friend and you know beyond a doubt that he's more than that; he's your Angel. He is so familiar to you! He's enormous, at least three times your size, and with a smile that's so reassuring that you feel it more than see it. He's so real and vibrant, in every detail. It's like he's lightening frozen into form. No, more like solid flames in a white-hot fire. There is such a silent excitement around you!

Now a strange sensation of being pulled toward him; but from behind you, a heavy sense, like thick, syrupy water parting from your form. Something has definitely separated itself from the back. You feel freed from the heaviness and slide joyously closer to your Guardian Angel. There's an awareness, an overwhelming air of emotion, like tranquility or gentle peace. But it's not around you, per se. You are part of it! It's inside of you. So nice; refreshing, like something you once knew, but somehow forgot. How?! How could anyone forget this? It's all so recent, so…perfect. A firm sense of goodness, or is it love? It's overpowering, like a fragrance. An inescapable fog of goodness, kindness, and some other emotion that's new, rushes through you. All of it is gushing quietly and calmly through your form, exhilarating every sense you thought you knew. It feels like you're grinning uncontrollably.

As you rise toward the Angel, an undeniable presence of safety and confidence securely grips you like a vice of velvet. It has a hold on you somehow, by the middle area, or from within maybe. Are you floating? There is definite movement though, of some kind. There's a flowing sensation, but no "wind." Thing's are passing by, and you're rising higher. You're moving together. Are you talking or listening? It's both. You know his name, but you don't know how you know. The stars gleam intensely all around. And then you're standing…before a great and massive door! It's mammoth! You're awed by how tiny and

insignificant you are in front of this door. The whole moment, up to this point, seems like a blink.

It slowly and silently swings inward and there He is! At the end of an aisle. It's Jesus, seated upon a glowing, thundering rainbow throne! You sense trembling as your Angel releases you. On either side of a long runway are millions upon millions of cheering saints – you know them all! You recognize every single face! But you're not facing them, yet you see them all. Your "eyes" are riveted upon the most absolutely divine face. It's Him – Jesus – sweet, wonderful King! He's magnificent!

As you near the throne, you're aware of the cheers from your friends. He rises to His feet and extends a hand…right to you! There's brassy music, soothing and silvery notes you've never even thought of that are like a memory, from childhood? No, before that. As a baby? Or maybe even before that, if that's possible. There's the scar on his wrist. The music, seemingly alive, pierces like a sword of brass and strings. You can't stand any longer, but you can't seem to fall either.

And then He speaks, audible words, like the golden crashes of a thousand waterfalls, *"WELL DONE, GOOD AND FAITHFUL SERVANT. ENTER INTO THE JOY OF YOUR FATHER."* What a voice, like your dear Mother, tender and firm. It radiates throughout the hall. A hush falls over everyone, hanging on the melody of God's pure voice. It seems to echo in your soul. Everything is right, so very right. It's as if you'd never been anywhere else. And so, we shall ever be…with the Lord of all, forever and ever.

His eyes, now glistening, look up from the trembling paper. The first real smile in weeks told me I'd jarred him back to the reality of what it means to be a true believer.

Death can be more exciting.

His door, on the way out, never swung so easy. And the busy hallways didn't really seem to smell that bad anymore. *"Oh, death, where is Thy sting?"* I thought. *"Where is Thy sting?"*

96

Week 48:
52 THANKS

"Kings will shut their mouths on account of Him (Isaiah 52:15)."

Can you remember something significant from 2016? After the last two years of Covid, normal memories seem to be buried pretty deep, let alone six years ago, but for me it's easy…that was the year I got paid to go to Israel to write 104 articles for the *Israel Ministry of Tourism*, and stood in Jerusalem (I'd have done it for free)!

They say that's a memory that you never forget, the first time you see Jerusalem. It was in January, like today, cold, windy, and snowing. That's also how long I've been writing this column, six years, and last month I combined some articles into a published book, a weekly devotional for the year for those still seeking Him called *52 Thinks About God*.

And so, it seemed appropriate to find a passage with "52" in it for today. Yesterday I read Isaiah chapter 52, which was divinely appropriate for mentioning a book about seeking God–who promises us He can be easily found (Jeremiah 29:12-13). This chapter in Isaiah is remarkable. It's a prophecy written around 700 B.C. about the future Messiah. It describes Him as a King, who will be badly beaten up (verses 13-15):

"Behold, My servant will prosper, He will be high and lifted up, and greatly exalted. Just as many were astonished at you, My people (Israel), so His appearance was marred more than the sons of men. Thus He will sprinkle many nations, Kings will shut their mouths on account of Him; for what had not been told them they will see, and what they had not heard they will understand."

This is not news to us Gentiles. The Christ will be a Jewish King who is rejected and killed, and *"sprinkle many nations"* with His blood. We know that story well, even if most don't believe it. Jesus of Nazareth was that King who died for our sins, and rose again from the dead, but to the Jews to whom Isaiah was writing, it was just plain crazy!

This Jewish King of all kings will be beaten to a bloody pulp, sprinkle other nations, and leave the rulers of the world dumbfounded? Sprinkling blood for sin was an easy concept to grasp from their sacrificial animal system in Jerusalem's Temple, but sprinkled with God's blood, from being beat up, from their promised Messiah-King?

So wait, Isaiah, are you saying this God-King would have human blood? Be fully human? This boggled Jewish minds, and still does today!

How can the God of Abraham be human, King, and die a bloody death, for all nations, even the Gentiles? Isn't He all-powerful? Who could sucker punch God-in-the-flesh? Isaiah explains it all in his next chapter, Isaiah 53, but first he says in 52:7, *"How lovely are the feet of those who bring good news."* That's the good news of my *52 Thinks* book.

Our suffering King came to save us all, to sprinkle our sins with His precious blood, and He will come again as the King of kings. That's very good news, worthy of 52 Thanks!

Week 49:
31,102

**"If you believed Moses, you would believe Me;
for he wrote of Me (John 5:46)."**

There's nothing like writing a perfect movie line. *"ET phone home."*
"Shaken, not stirred." "Adrian!" "I'll be back." "Feel lucky, punk?"
"Frankly, my dear, I don't give a damn." "I'm your huckleberry."

For a writer, that's the cherry on top of a good script, especially if it's the
very last line, like in *The Apartment* film: *"Well, nobody's perfect."*

I try to come up with one when I'm writing all the time – a great line that
will live forever in Hollywood, and the shorter, the better. Here's a few
favorites, in three words or less:

The Blind Side: A very wealthy Sandra Bullock shows their adopted son
from the street his new bedroom. He's stunned, says he never had one
before, so she asks, *"What? A room to yourself?"* Looking down at it,
with pitiful puppy eyes, Michael says, *"A bed."*

Hoosiers: Basketball coach Gene Hackman tells Buddy to play good
defense in the game, and stick with their best player like chewing gum.
When Buddy comes back to the bench after a successful stint, he says to
Hackman with a straight face, *"It was Dentyne."*

Casablanca: A mysterious Rick answers Louis as to why he's in
Casablanca, but Rick doesn't want to reveal his past, so he says he came
for the waters. Louis corrects him with, *"We're in the desert."* Without
missing a beat, Bogie says, *"I was misinformed."*

The Undefeated: John Wayne exposes two shady Federal horse agents
as thieves, and when the big one goes for his gun, Wayne slugs him. The
smaller crook pleads, *"I didn't do anything."* The Duke says, *"You should
have."* Then punches him in the face.

Jesus has a memorable line too. Well, He had a lot of them, since He
wrote the Bible, but there's one three-word line in the 31,102 verses in the

Bible that really nails His life's mission. Any guesses what it is? There's a hint in the Book of Hebrews, chapter 10.

Israel tried to keep the Law of Moses, to be made right with God, to deal with their sin by blood (Leviticus 17:11), but it was never intended as a permanent solution (that's why they did it every year). The Temple, the sacrifices, and their Feasts were reminders that they needed forgiveness, *"Well, nobody's perfect,"* all symbols pointing to the Messiah.

These temporary sacrifices were finished, *"once for all time,"* when the Passover Lamb was not an animal, but a perfect God-man. As John the Baptizer said when he saw Jesus, *"Behold, the Lamb of God who takes away the sins of the world."* That's His mission.

All Jewish blood sacrifices for sin ended when Rome destroyed the Temple in 70 A.D. According to the Law of Moses without shedding blood all sin remains, but the good news is that it's not needed if you take Jesus' sacrifice as your own. Now, can you guess His famous three-word line? Just give up and it'll all make perfect sense (John 19:30).

Week 50:
You're (Not) Welcome Here

"Because there was no room for them in the inn (Luke 2:7)."

John Hughes wrote a brilliant film that we always fit in on Thanksgiving. *Home Alone* (a brat is accidentally left behind on his family's vacation) has a clever scene chocked-full of subtext...a finally repentant Kevin is in church on Christmas Eve and meets his scary neighbor, Old Man Marley, the legendary and unfounded, *"South Bend Shovel Slayer."*

But Kevin is shocked; Marley is actually nice! He asks the boy if he's "been good." Kevin comes clean and admits he's feeling bad, hence his visit. *"I've been kind of a pain lately. I said some things I shouldn't have. I really haven't been too good this year."*

Marley then tells Kevin he's there to watch his granddaughter's choir rehearsal because he can't come hear her tonight. *"I'm not welcome,"* he says. A stunned Kevin asks, *"At church?"* Marley explains his estranged relationship with his son and how they haven't spoken in years, but assures Kevin that *"you're always welcome at church."* Amen.

The subtext is as deep as the manure in the Bethlehem stall where Jesus ended up after being rejected...Kevin confesses his guilt (just like Marley and his son need to do). That's the "corncrib to cross" Bethlehem manger story. We're all separated by our Kevin-like rebellion (Isaiah 59:2), and despite our obvious guilt, we don't welcome the Savior's arrival, even when He came to save us. As the innkeeper said, *"No room."*

On this Christmas Eve you may feel "not welcome" in church, in God's presence. Your sin and regrets do separate you from your Father. That estrangement is genuine (Isaiah 53:6), but the truth is that His love is unaffected, quite literally...stable. Like Kevin's admission, you'll find empathy and forgiveness if you call on Him (Romans 10:13).

Consider Paul's words in Romans chapter 5: *"But God demonstrates His own love toward us, in that while we were yet sinners, Christ died for us. Much more then, having been justified by His blood, we shall be saved from the wrath of God through Him. For if while we were enemies, we were reconciled to God through the death of His Son, much more, having been reconciled, we shall be saved by His life."*

God didn't just say He loved us – He demonstrated it. He jumped into our goldfish bowl, and became a goldfish. Filthy water, like Bethlehem's stall (and our own cruddy hearts filled with sin and regrets and steamy crap) didn't matter. Jesus came anyway, died when we were enemies, and shed His blood to save us from what we deserved…God's wrath.

This reconciliation is in the past tense. He already did it. You just need to repent (apologize) and make room in your heart-stall. His Christmas gift is bought and paid for and free. Just receive Him (John 1:12). He loves crappy stalls and dirty goldfish bowls. Now go watch the *Home Alone* ending with Marley and his son. A welcome sight!

Week 51:
A Tale of Two Cities

"For David, after he had served the purpose of God in his own generation, fell asleep... (Acts 13:36)."

October 29th is a rough day. On that day, in 1978, my brother Jack committed suicide. And on that day, this year, my friend and Pastor dropped dead. Mike was as an avid biker and in great shape. The suddenness stung. In remembering them, Charles Dickens' first line from our title seems to fit, *"It was the best of times, it was the worst of times."*

So why Mike? The Davidic answer is simple...because Mike had served God's purpose. Have you considered your purpose? Why you're here? When you'll leave? Most of us never do. We may order a drink after a bike ride in a local coffee shop, and think we'll walk out. We never think this is my final act and collapse at the counter. Mike did that.

Two precious souls entered eternity on the same date. Jack was born once, but as a Christian, Mike was born twice (John 3:3). Both losses made me incredibly sad, but the latter was like King David who only "fell asleep." Mike is only napping. Jack, I'm afraid, never accepted Jesus Christ as his Lord and Savior. I hope I'm wrong, but evidence for faith should be blatant (like Mike's life) and not requiring a microscope.

Death is so final, so impartial. If you've lost a loved one, you know. I found this poem in Mike's office (he bookmarked the page). It's written by Henry Van Dyke (*Gone From My Sight*), aptly re-named in this grief book, *Gone Where?* I hope it helps comfort you.

Imagine you are standing on the seashore. A ship at your side spreads her white sails to the morning breeze and starts for the blue ocean. She is an object of beauty and strength and you stand and watch her until at length she hangs like a speck of white cloud just where the sea and sky meet and mingle with each other:

"There, she is gone."

Gone where? Gone from your sight, that is all. She is just as large in hull and mast and spar as when she left your side and just as able to bear her

load of living freight to the place of her destination. Her diminished size is in you, not in her.

And just at the moment when someone at your side says, "She's gone," there are other eyes watching for her coming and other voices ready to take up the glad shout, "Here she comes!" And this is what we call dying — this is life (in Christ Jesus)!

This comforts me because Mike (who had his sin removed, 2 Corinthians 5:21) met Jesus immediately on that shore and is very much alive. That's the good news. We can all look forward to death and the resurrection if we have trusted Christ and repented, as Paul wrote, *"There is therefore now no condemnation for those who are in Christ Jesus (Romans 8:1)."* That word *"now"* always rings a little louder when I slip up.

"Now" is an exact word. Very close to "know." In seconds, you can now be beyond the horizon too. It's inevitable. But your destination can be a certainty. You can know for sure you're going to Heaven (1 John 5:11-13). Mike gave a sermon once with Dickens' *A Tale of Two Cities* as his title and it reminded me of another Dickens' story with an equally famous opening line, where death is a start, *"Marley was dead, to begin with."*

Later in the story, Scrooge says, *"Mr. Marley has been dead these seven years. He died seven years ago, this very night."* That's exactly what Jesus said, *"This very night...your soul is required of you (Luke 12:20)."* Three haunting words we should take to heart. A North Carolina nobody, who became America's most famous evangelist, did exactly that.

Billy Graham said, *"Someday you will read or hear that Billy Graham is dead. Don't you believe a word of it. I shall be more alive than I am now. I will have just changed my address. I will have gone into the presence of God."* Your now is coming, but it can be the best of times, if you know His now, *"There is therefore now no condemnation..."*

Death can be a great start, *"to begin with,"* a great opening line, *"the best of times,"* in your own tale of two cities, of two residences, if you change addresses with Billy and Mike, their shouts will be *"Here she comes!"*

Week 52:
But God

"And without faith it is impossible to please God, for he who comes to God must believe that He is, and that He is a rewarder of those who seek Him (Hebrews 11:6)."

"Men to the left, women to the right. Men to the left, women to the right."

Indifference. That was the blasé tone of the Nazi commands to the Jews at the *Auschwitz* train depot. Hate implies some emotion exists, but indifference has no feeling at all.

Indifference also typifies our view of God. If we're honest, we don't care if He's real. You may contest that, but a true litmus test of what you love is your expenditure of time and money (Matthew 6:21). If He's real, the greatest Being ever, and loves you, then it's stupefying that we ignore Him; but then again, a corpse is pretty hard to impress.

The Bible says that's because we're dead, a spiritual corpse, a dead soul, which explains our lackadaisical God attitude. Sin killed it and us. *"And you were dead in your trespasses and sins (Ephesians 2:1)."* A disinterest in seeking God confirms this truth, *"no one seeks God (Romans 3:11)."* Deep down, we don't trust Him to have our best interests at heart, so we dismiss Him. But God, thankfully, cared, and loved us anyway.

God puts a supreme value on trust, what the Bible calls Faith, the *"conviction of things not seen (Hebrews 11:1)."* He gave us a wake up-nudge when He became a man, and Jesus reaffirmed faith's importance, asking us to believe that He and the Father were one and the same. So why does a loving God put a premium on trust and faith?

Trust is the core of a relationship. It implies a dependency, and in this case that He knows better than we do, *"a rewarder of those who seek Him."* As a father, I want my child's trust when I tell them to do something, or to avoid something dangerous, to believe that I instruct them out of love. To question me is heartbreaking. To ignore me is even worse, but if I love them then I must let them choose to obey me, and to trust me.

So it is with our heavenly Father who says sin separates us from Him (Isaiah 59:2). Our indifference confirms it; we don't believe Him. But God, despite our hurtful attitude, not only said He loves us, He demonstrated it when He died for our sins. He came after us, even though we didn't care (Luke 19:10). Jesus knew that, and He still came. When God "butted in," it meant His Son would die, for you, and yet most of us still ignore Him.

Romans 5:8 says, *"But God demonstrates His own love for us in that while we were yet sinners, Christ died for us."* And Ephesians 2:4-5, *"But God being rich in mercy, because of the great love with which He loved us, even when we were dead in our trespasses, made us alive together with Christ."* But God – two words to change your life's direction, if you trust Him, *"a rewarder of those who seek Him."*

Or just stay indifferent, as His love allows you to choose to do. *"Men to the left, women to the right. Men to the left, women to the right."*

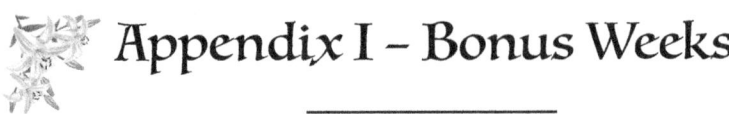

Appendix I – Bonus Weeks

Bonus Week 1:
Precious

"Lead on! The night is waning fast, and it is precious time to me."

So says a now fully aware Ebenezer Scrooge to his last visitor, a Grim Reaper apparition who is unmistakably Death himself. Like a masked executioner, Scrooge pleads with him to be quick, and calls his dwindling time "precious."

Precious isn't used much now, but a fitting description as the currency slipping through his stingy fingers is the only commodity Death trades in – Time. Do not miss Dickens' meaning. This Phantom is taking a life, and specifically, Scrooge is tonight's transaction.

Charles Dickens' *A Christmas Carol* is, word for word, the one holiday story you should read before you die. It is brilliantly brief, but do not mistake his lean writing for folly…it is timeless, pregnant with genius, and his reclamation tale takes only two hours to read!

So, what exactly is precious…to you?

Think hard on that. Decide what is your most precious thing, and then consider how to safeguard it. If you're honest you'll see it can only be Time, and like Scrooge you are losing it…right now, this very minute slips away.

And what would God (who is outside of Time) consider precious? He says our faith in Jesus and His dripping blood (1 Peter 1:7 and 19), His promises (2 Peter 1:4), His love (Psalm 36:7), and the death of his godly ones (Psalm 116:15). These all fit hand and glove into Dickens' choice, and bring to mind two other precious-conscious writers.

In Tolkien's *The Lord of the Rings*, Gollum calls his magic Ring "Precious," and its power transforms his desire into deadly lust and

corrupts him. Sin changes him into a horrific monster, as it does to us. Thankfully, Tolkien's friend, C.S. Lewis persuaded the doubtful author to publish his Hobbit tale, and then Lewis wrote of another "Precious."

"It is a serious thing to live in a society of possible gods and goddesses, to remember that the dullest most uninteresting person you can talk to may one day be a creature which, if you saw it now, you would be strongly tempted to worship, or else a horror and a corruption such as you now meet, if at all, only in a nightmare. All day long we are, in some degree helping each other to one or the other of these destinations. It is in light of these overwhelming possibilities, it is with the awe and the circumspection proper to them, that we should conduct all of our dealings with one another, all friendships, all loves, all play, all politics. There are no ordinary people. You have never talked to a mere mortal. Nations, cultures, arts, and civilizations–these are mortal, and their life is to ours as the life of a gnat. But it is immortals whom we joke with, work with, marry, snub, and exploit–immortal horrors or everlasting splendors." Souls are precious too.

Dickens got it right. Time is precious, and the holidays remind us of that, but Lewis reminds us that only Jesus can help us get more Time, through faith in His precious blood sacrifice you get life eternal. And that's what *Ebenezer* means in Hebrew, Stone of Help, a very precious stone.

Bonus Week 2:
Can You Ϭusrϲ the Blbie?

"Ϭbis is the judgmenϲ, that the Light has come into the world, and men loved the darkness rather than the Light, for their deeds were evil (John 3:19)."

The phaonmneal pweor of the huamn mnid, aoccdrnig to Cmabrigde Uinervtisy rsceeacrh, syas it deosn't mttaer in waht oredr the ltteers in a wrod are arnarged, the olny iprmoatnt tihng is taht the fsirt and lsat ltteer be in the rghit pclae.

The rset can be a taotl mses and you wlil sltil raed it wouthit a porbelm.

Tihs is bcuseae the huamn mnid deos not raed ervey lteter, but the wrod as a wlohe.

Amzanig, huh? Bleeive me?

Our nepswaper clumon lsat mnoth daelt wtih the autthoiry of the Blbie and wehtehr or not God wluod alolw sotehming as criitcal as His supneraturlaly reealved insrtucnstios to us for our etnreal savlaiton bieng oepn to consfuion, tapmernig, or miinsterprteatoin. Eevn in tihs prupesfluly miexd up cloumn, we stlil get the mian piont of tihs mesasge.

How mcuh mroe so if the Amligthy God watned to comumniacte His soltuion for our suols to dael with sin and detah? Wulod God alolw any ctnoamiantion to His mesasge? Wloud He mkae it hrad to unedrtasnd? Is He pwoerufl enuogh to ptroect His wrods?

Thsee are obivosuly rhetociral qusteions. Of coruse God is storng enoguh to procett His svlaation meassge. The rael quetison is actulaly a matetr of the haert…are you wlliing to reveice His measgse by rediang the Bilbe for yosruelf?

Look waht Jeuss siad in Luke 16:31, "But He said to him, 'If they do not listen to Moses and the Prophets, they will not be persuaded even if someone rises from the dead.'" If tehy wolud not acecpt the

messgae of the Old Tetsamnet rergading tiehr sin and His lvoe for tehm, eevn afetr sieeng so mnay demontsratoins of His mirauclous lvoe, eevn rasiing the daed wluod not sotfen tehir hrad heatrs. It's not crebidility...it's stubbnroess.

Your hrad herat, lvoe of slef, and sin, preevnts you form eevn reanidg His Wrod. So lte's hvae no mroe excsues abuot the Bbile bieng flul of conrtadicitons or mistinerprteatoins. The rael isuse is yuor haert and you simlpy dno't lvoe God.

Or myabe yuo're afarid, like a naghuty chlid who feras dispciline, but tihs is precilsey why Jeuss cmae...to tkae yuor puhnsiment, so you colud cmoe bcak. Lkie the Prdoigal Son stroy taht Jseus tlod in Luke 15, yuor Fatehr lnogs for you to cmoe hmoe.

Wlil you gvie up and adimt yuor need (Isaiah 64:6), or mkae lmae exucses aoubt the Bilbe's inipsration. Hvae you eevn seriolsuy raed the Bblie? Why not try rdaeing the Gospel of John and see for yruoslef if Jeuss is the olny way as He clamied (John 14:6)? You mgiht fnid taht He loevs you, and olny watns to hlep you. Eevn miexd up, lkie this cloumn, if yuo'll just raed His Wrod you may fnid taht He loevs you. If not, tehn mabye yuo're the rael contracidtion for criticizing soemthing yuo've not seirously reda and it's not the Blibe...or pehraps you jsut lvoe the dkraness?

110

Bonus Week 3:
Do Staples Float?

"When they arrived at the Jordan, they began cutting down trees. But as one of them was cutting a tree, his ax head fell into the river. 'Oh, sir!' he cried. 'It was a borrowed ax!' 'Where did it fall?' the man of God asked. When he showed him the place, Elisha cut a stick and threw it into the water at that spot. Then the ax head floated to the surface. 'Grab it,' Elisha said. And the man reached out and grabbed it (2 Kings 6)."

I've heard this excuse many times. *"If God is real, why doesn't He just appear to me here, right now, then I'd believe."* In other words, prove it, impress me, make an ax head float. The great King Herod wanted Jesus to do parlor tricks for him, but Jesus declined. Jesus knew that even rising from the dead wouldn't grab a hard heart (Luke 16:19-31).

God is not a trained monkey doing dog and pony shows on our whims. His marvelous deeds are recorded in the Bible for all to read, from a victory parade through a bone-dry Red Sea to an empty tomb near Jerusalem. *"Moses and the Prophets"* are enough for a soft heart, but sometimes He gives us a tiny glimpse that He really is *"here, right now."*

On August 8-9, 1942, at only 19, Elgin Staples was blown overboard when Japanese cruisers near Guadalcanal attacked his ship. Despite shrapnel in his shoulder and both legs, his lifebelt kept him afloat for four frantic hours fighting not to be swept out to sea.

"I began treading water, trying to stay calm as I felt things brush against my legs, knowing that if a shark attacked me, any moment could be my last."

When he was safely onboard a third ship (he was rescued, returned to his ship, but it was too badly damaged and sank), he examined the M1926 inflatable lifebelt and saw that it was made in Akron, Ohio at the *Firestone Tire and Rubber Company*…his hometown! He decided to keep the lifebelt as a souvenir. Eventually he got sent home to recuperate.

"After a quietly emotional welcome, I sat with my mother in our kitchen, telling her about my recent ordeal and hearing what had happened at home since I had gone away. My mother informed me that 'to do her part,' she had gotten a wartime job at the Firestone plant. Surprised, I jumped up and grabbing my life belt from my duffel bag, put it on the table in front of her.

'Take a look at that, Mom,' I said, 'It was made right here in Akron, at your plant.'

She leaned forward and taking the rubber belt in her hands, she read the label. She had just heard the story and knew that in the darkness of that terrible night, it was this one piece of rubber that had saved my life. When she looked up at me, her mouth and her eyes were open wide with surprise. 'Son, I'm an inspector at Firestone. This is my inspector number,' she said, her voice hardly above a whisper.

We stared at each other, too stunned to speak. Then I stood up, walked around the table and pulled her up from her chair. We held each other in a tight embrace, saying nothing. My mother was not a demonstrative woman, but the significance of this amazing coincidence overcame her usual reserve. We hugged each other for a long, long time, feeling the bond between us. My mother had put her arms halfway around the world to save me."

Is this a huge reach, just a crazy coincidence? Maybe. I did not plan to write this column today, but is it a coincidence that today is the 80th anniversary of our victory in World War II? Maybe. But if you asked Vera Staples, who prayed for her boy 8,000 miles away, I know what she'd say. Coincidence is God's way of remaining anonymous.

Now ask yourself this…what are the odds, that God did all that, over 80 years ago, and indeed rose from the dead 2,000 years ago to be your lifebelt, *"here, right now,"* just to get your attention by reading this today? I know what Elisha would say, *"Grab it!"*

112

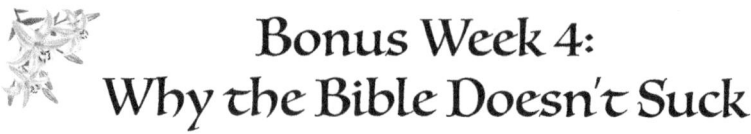

Bonus Week 4:
Why the Bible Doesn't Suck

"All Scripture is inspired by God...(2 Timothy 3:16)."

My mom always told me to read the Bible, the number one bestseller of all-time.

It had great stuff in it she promised…wars, sex, murder, giants, miracles, angels, and demons. But is it reliable as God's Word to speak to us today? Let's look at just the New Testament, and the two primary questions that guide linguistic scholar's textual criticisms:

• How many copies are there to examine and compare?

• How close in time are the oldest copies to the originals?

The more copies that exist, and the closer in time the copies are to the original, the more accurate the results. Ancient works like Josephus or Thucydides are rarely questioned as being authentic in authorship or content, but Josephus has only nine copies and Thucydides has just eight copies.

All the other major works of note from ancient history such as Plato (7), Caesar (10), Pliny (7), Euripides (9), Tacitus (20), and Herodotus (8) are 20 copies or less, and usually much less! Only Sophocles (193) and Aristotle (49) have more than 20.

The New Testament has almost 25,000 copies!

The next closest document would be Homer's *Iliad* with 643 copies with a 500-year gap. Ironically, none of these other manuscripts are contested, despite an 800 – 2,000 year gap from the originals to the copies.

Conversely, one piece of John's gospel is dated to within 25 years after the original was written!

Sir Frederic Kenyon, former director of the British Museum, said, *"In no other case is the interval of time between the composition of the book and the date of the earliest manuscripts so short as in that*

of the New Testament. The last foundation for any doubt that the Scriptures have come down to us substantially as they were written has now been removed."

More importantly, these New Testament copies have a 99.5% accuracy rate!

New Testament specialist Daniel Wallace says there are about 300,000 individual variations of the text of the New Testament, but that this number is very misleading. Most of the differences are inconsequential--spelling errors, inverted phrases and the like. A side-by-side comparison between the two main text families (the Majority Text and the Modern Critical Text) shows agreement at a full 98% of the time.

Of the remaining differences, virtually all yield to vigorous textual criticism. This means that our New Testament is 99.5% textually pure. In the entire text of 20,000 lines, only 40 lines are in doubt (about 400 words), and none affects any significant doctrine!

Greek scholar D.A. Carson sums it up this way: *"The purity of text is of such a substantial nature that nothing we believe to be true, and nothing we are commanded to do, is in any way jeopardized by the variants."*

So if God authored the Bible, and He meant it to be His primary communication device to us, do you think He would, as the all-powerful Creator of life, supernaturally protect its contents...to communicate a message to you?

Bonus Week 5:
Why the Bible Doesn't Suck II

"All Scripture is inspired by God...(2 Timothy 3:16)."

Last time we discussed the credibility of the New Testament. Now we'll consider the Old Testament's viability as God's primary communication to us.

In 1947, a Bedouin teenager crawled into a cave in Qumran, Israel and found some clay jars that he hoped were filled with treasure. What he found was just some old scrolls, but they turned out to be more valuable than treasure and launched an 11-year search that produced almost 900 manuscripts.

It was the largest biblical manuscript discovery of all time! They ranged from full scrolls (almost 28 feet long) to fragments written in Hebrew, Greek, and Aramaic on papyrus, parchment, and bronze. Every one of the 39 Old Testament books was represented, except the Book of Esther.

The scrolls were also the oldest manuscripts ever found! Before this find, the oldest was dated to 1008 A.D. The oldest Qumran scroll is from about 250 B.C. and the latest to 68 A.D., which is exciting because the closer to the time of the manuscript's origins and the actual event recorded, the more reliable the text (a huge corroborating factor in ancient textual criticism). This was more than a 1,000-year leap!

Together, as the largest and oldest find, these scrolls were pure archaeological gold because when compared with current manuscripts, they confirmed the reliability of the Old Testament in dramatic similarity. To fully appreciate this find, and its precision in content, we need to understand the two primary questions for linguistic scholars:

• How many copies are there to examine and compare?

• How close in time are the oldest copies to the originals?

So the more copies that exist and the closer in time they are to the original, the more accurate the results. Consider these famously accepted and reliable ancient works:

Josephus has nine copies (400 years later) and Thucydides has eight copies (1,300 years later). Plato (7), Caesar (10), Pliny (7), Euripides (9), Tacitus (20), and Herodotus (8) are 20 copies or less. Only Homer's *Iliad* (643), Sophocles (193), and Aristotle (49) have more than 20 copies.

The Old Testament has over 10,000 copies and the Qumran scrolls now move the date to only 150 years after the event–Malachi in 400 B.C. In literary circles, this is not only unheard of, but pure gold for reliability! Unbelievably, there's even more supernatural evidence in the content of these 10,000 copies.

When comparing the Dead Sea Scrolls and the oldest previous texts from 1008 A.D., it is basically a perfect match! This incredible detail over centuries proves that the copying methods used by the scribes were very sophisticated and successful.

They had numerical systems to ensure each page was exact. They counted the number of lines, letters, and words per page of the new copy and then checked them with the original. If they didn't match perfectly, they destroyed the copy.

So why did God supernaturally author and protect the Bible? Perhaps He has something important to say to you…personally. Maybe cracking open a Bible and reading some of it, say the Gospel of John or Luke, is a good idea. I'll wager you'll find more than Bedouin treasure.

Bonus Week 6:
Drop Dead!

"And inasmuch as it is appointed for men to die once and after this comes judgment (Hebrews 9:27)."

That's my Easter message to you. No chocolate bunnies or candy eggs.

I mean we're all going to do that some day, so why not use it as a greeting this Easter? Walk into church on Sunday and with a big smile, let'em have it with gusto:

"Drop dead!"

Let me explain. This verse in the Book of Hebrews makes it crystal clear that there is no reincarnation, no purgatory, and no other escape from His righteous judgment.

We will all die, and then a righteous and unerring Judge will judge all of us. Simple theology. His criteria? He Himself is the standard (Matthew 5:48). Absolute perfection. Holiness.

Utter and glaring bright righteousness where not one sin, mistake, or error will be squinted at. Anything less than absolute perfect morality will be judged wanting. Think about it. If God let us sinners into His Heaven it'd be the same mess we have now on earth, right?

Can't have sin in Heaven. Sin has to be eliminated to have holiness.

But on the other hand, nobody's perfect, right? We've all broken a commandment or two. Everyone has stolen something or lied or dishonored parents. So how is this fair if we all fall short of His perfect standard? Seems rigged. Shouldn't He weigh our good deeds against our bad deeds? Nope. That's not perfect and absolute 100 % holiness.

As James said, *"For whoever keeps the whole law and yet stumbles in one point, he has become guilty of all (James 2:10)."*

That's the bad news. According to James, we are all guilty of breaking all the commandments because just one sin kills perfection. Now

here's the good news that makes Easter the greatest holiday of all time…we don't have to stay dead as Jesus proved when He left His grave EMPTY!

That's our guarantee that death and punishment can be taken care of, a substitute takes all of our righteous judgment for sin for us, as Peter said, *"For Christ also died for sins once for all, the just for the unjust, so that He might bring us to God, having been put to death in the flesh, but made alive in the spirit* (1 Peter 3:18)."

The only catch is in Mark 1:14-15, *"Repent and believe."*

Repent is a fancy word for changing your mind. Instead of going left, you go right. Instead of ham, you chose liver for Easter dinner. Also known as surrendering, admitting you're defeated and lost. Instead of doing what you want, you surrender to what He wants…all of it.

And believing isn't in your head. It's in your heart. It means action. You do it because you believe it. You take a stand, like getting baptized; something He wants and your first proof of believing (Matthew 28:18-20). Symbolically you "drop dead" into the water, and come up out of "death" like Jesus Christ…a new and forgiven person by faith in His death and resurrection…with your own empty grave in the water.

So have a Happy Easter, have some liver for dinner, and drop dead…please!

Appendix II – My Story

Tough Questions

The bedroom door flew open. My oldest brother stood in the doorway sobbing. "Phillip! Wake up. Jack's dead. He's killed himself. He blew himself up in his car with gasoline." I had never before seen my brother cry, but I watched him walk away that night sobbing uncontrollably. Both shocked and sad, I sat there wondering one question...why? Why did my brother Jack kill himself?

After the funeral, still another question haunted me...where was my brother Jack now? The body that we placed in the ground was nothing more than a clay shell. The things that had made Jack a person were no longer there. He was gone. One day he was alive, living in Los Angeles. The next day, I found myself struggling to see his scarred features through a plastic body bag. I realized at that moment just how temporary life really is.

Footsteps

I admired Jack more than anyone else I knew. He was a big, muscular guy---tough with the men and charming with the ladies. He had earned my respect as a fighter in high school, with his "black leather jacket" image and "James Dean" charisma. All through school, I imitated him and followed in his footsteps. Jack was cool and I wanted to be just like him. He seemed to have it totally together...and then he died. What could have made him so hopeless that he'd take his own life? All I had was questions. It wasn't until my freshman year at Michigan State that I finally got some answers.

3 a.m.

It all started with a question that a guy in my dorm asked me one day: "If you died tonight and stood before God, and He asked you why He should let you into His Heaven, what would you say?" It was a pretty

heavy question and I was somewhat taken off guard. I wasn't used to being asked such direct questions about God, so I rattled off some "conditioned" response about God's love and forgiveness. But even after I had left his room thinking that I had successfully evaded his question, I couldn't forget it. It dug deep into my conscience. When you experience a death as close as your own brother, you can't help but wonder about God. The reality of death is no longer a "maybe someday." All of a sudden it hits you head on, right in the face!

As the school term wore on, I thought about that guy's question more and more honestly. My brother's death had forced me to realistically evaluate my life, and without excuses. I began to see that I was not "cool," not with God anyway. It really hit me one morning about three o'clock, during a party on our dorm floor. I went down to that guy's room again and woke him up. I was pretty incoherent from partying, as well as scared, but I managed to mumble something about wanting to talk about God. I was scared because I finally admitted to myself for the first time where I thought I was going. No one had to tell me. My life spoke loud and clear.

Once inside the room I told him that I wasn't sure where I would go when I died, but that I wanted to be positive. He still wasn't quite awake, but invited me inside to talk. He showed me a verse in the Bible that said that it was possible to know for certain. "These things I have written to you who believe in the name of the Son of God, in order that you may know that you have eternal life." He explained to me that none of us could naturally be in Heaven with God because He is perfect. No matter how good we have been, we all fall short of God's standard of perfection. That was no news to me. I knew I wasn't perfect---far from it. The Bible calls this condition Sin, which he explained was a Greek archery term for an arrow that had failed to hit the center of the target. But sin is also a very dangerous and lethal thing. Because of it we can't enjoy a relationship with God. "For whoever keeps the whole law and yet stumbles in one point, he has

become guilty of all." If we die in this condition of sin, we are not only separated from Him in this life, but for all eternity. "Your sins have made a separation between you and your God."

"...And Justice for All"

Now even though I knew that I wasn't perfect, I had a hard time believing that a loving God would throw me into Hell. One analogy, however, helped me to see that God's character was more than just love. Imagine that I am arrested for drunk driving after losing control of my car and had killed two pedestrians. Later, when my case came up in court, I discovered that the judge was my very own father! Even though my father loves me, as a judge he must punish me to fulfill his duty and obey the law. If he let me off the hook, he would not be just. The families of the people that I had killed would demand justice for my actions. The parallel is clear. Although God loves us, He must punish sin or else He would no longer be righteous. The point is that we are not good enough for a holy God to accept us into Heaven. Our sin cannot be swept under the carpet; it must be dealt with righteously. It was then that I realized that I had a warped concept of God. I had always assumed that when I asked for forgiveness, I got it merely because I asked, but I was never assured of it. How then was I to be forgiven?

God actually became a man, Jesus Christ, in order to satisfy the wrath our sin deserved by dying on the cross. Since God demands a perfect payment for sin, and none of us is perfect, the only one that could pay for our sin was God Himself. "He made Him (Jesus) who knew no sin to become sin on our behalf that we might become the righteousness of God in Him." God's love and justice merged at the cross. But I already believed these things that he was telling me. What was I missing?

Action!

If I told you that I put a rattlesnake in your bed, would you sleep there that night? Of course not if you believed me. Real faith, a real saving-eternal faith, involves action. If you really believe something, then you'll act on it. I realized that though I intellectually agreed with these facts, I had never acted on them. It was simply head knowledge. So that night, I admitted to God that I was a sinner and needed His forgiveness. I freely gave God control of my life and made Him my Lord, promising to follow and obey because of what He had done for me. Even though I had chosen to be indifferent with God, my brother's death forced me to answer some tough questions. What made my brother so hopeless was that he had chosen to ignore Christ's payment for his sin. All he had to hope in was in this life and it never satisfied him. Are you satisfied? I'd like to challenge you to consider today whether or not you're positive that you're going to Heaven. If you're not sure, I'd love to talk to you.

A special thanks to Amy, Leah, Dan, Jeremy, Kailee, Emily, Dale, Patty, and DW (and the Choo-Bear for sleeping with it). I am grateful to each of you for your encouragements and taking the time to read my columns before going to press, so I only look dumb (and not sound dumb too).

And thanks to all of you who have in the spirit of "Elf on the Shelf" taken a copy on your travels around the world and then given it away, after sending me a picture (Emily and Dale, Bill and Kathe, Rob and Kim, Johnny and Lisa, Dan and Dawn, Lucia, Sharon, and Peg…who took it to see Bob Dylan!).

And to Peter for his hard work putting this together, tiny edits, and designing the cover, Bill and Chris for double-checking me, and Gary for his very kind words about my words, and above all…

Aslan, the firstborn from the dead, who spared my life, and gave me His words (I am not competent). This book is my thank you to You, and like Reepicheep of Narnia, and J. Alec Motyer who said it so very well, "I lay my sword-pen at your feet."

Made in the USA
Middletown, DE
12 October 2025